KV

BLOODY ROADS TO GERMANY

BLOODY ROADS TO GERMANY

At Huertgen Forest and the Bulge—
An American Soldier's Courageous
Story of World War II

WILLIAM F. MELLER

BERKLEY CALIBER, NEW YORK

BERKLEY BOOKS
Published by the Penguin Group
Penguin Group (USA) Inc.
375 Hudson Street, New York, New York 10014, USA
Penguin Group (Canada), 90 Eglinton Avenue East, Suite 700, Toronto, Ontario M4P 2Y3, Canada
(a division of Pearson Penguin Canada Inc.) • Penguin Books Ltd., 80 Strand, London WC2R 0RL,
England • Penguin Group Ireland, 25 St. Stephen's Green, Dublin 2, Ireland (a division of Penguin
Books Ltd.) • Penguin Group (Australia), 250 Camberwell Road, Camberwell, Victoria 3124, Australia
(a division of Pearson Australia Group Pty. Ltd.) • Penguin Books India Pvt. Ltd., 11 Community
Centre, Panchsheel Park, New Delhi—110 017, India • Penguin Group (NZ), 67 Apollo Drive,
Rosedale, Auckland 0632, New Zealand (a division of Pearson New Zealand Ltd.) • Penguin Books
(South Africa) (Pty.) Ltd., 24 Sturdee Avenue, Rosebank, Johannesburg 2196, South Africa

Penguin Books Ltd., Registered Offices: 80 Strand, London WC2R 0RL, England

This book is an original publication of The Berkley Publishing Group.

The publisher does not have any control over and does not assume any responsibility
for author or third-party websites or their content.

FIRST EDITION: December 2012

Library of Congress Cataloging-in-Publication Data

Meller, William F.
Bloody roads to Germany : at Huertgen Forest and the Bulge :
an American soldier's courageous story of World War II / by William F. Meller.
p.   cm.
ISBN 978-0-425-25961-0
1. Meller, William F.   2. Ardennes, Battle of the, 1944–1945—Personal narratives, American.
3. United States. Army. Infantry Division 28th.   4. Soldiers—United States—Biography.   I. Title.
D756.5.A7M38 2012
940.54'219348092—dc23
[B]
2012029273

PRINTED IN THE UNITED STATES OF AMERICA

10 9 8 7 6 5 4 3 2 1

Penguin is committed to publishing works of quality and integrity.
In that spirit, we are proud to offer this book to our readers;
however, the story, the experiences, and the words are the author's alone.

ALWAYS LEARNING   PEARSON

For my father; he was the first:

EDWARD E. MELLER, CORPORAL, 1917–1919

3rd Platoon, I Company, 110th Regiment, 28th Infantry Division. Silver Star, Purple Heart, European Campaign Medal, three Battle Stars, Battle of Champagne-Marne, Battle of Aisne-Marne, and Battle of Defensive Sector Pennsylvania National Guard Medal, Victory Medal

WILLIAM F. MELLER, STAFF SERGEANT, 1943–1945

2nd Platoon, I Company, 110th Regimental Combat Team, 28th Infantry Division. Combat Infantry Badge, Bronze Star, Prisoner-of-War Medal, European Campaign Medal, three Battle Stars (Battle of Rhineland, Battle of Ardennes, Battle of Central Europe), Unit Citation, Good Conduct Medal, American Campaign Medal, Victory Medal

Edward E. Meller's and William F. Meller's U.S. Army Medals.

ACKNOWLEDGMENTS

My warmest acknowledgments to executive editor Natalee Rosenstein for gathering the pieces, then creating a winner; you are a true professional.

To Natalee's assistant, Robin Barletta, who made me feel "something special" in this unfamiliar world: You were never too busy. That made it work.

My thanks to agent E. J. McCarthy: With your vast knowledge you sold the work, then nudged this author along the right path.

Marilyn Quigly, professor of creative writing and author, I appreciate your constantly telling me I should be published. It stayed with me.

John McManus, professor of history and author: You held your hand on my shoulder throughout this journey to save me from my mistakes.

Robert F. Phillips, U.S. Army historian: Your verification of official statistics and accuracies gave this work the credibility it deserves.

Michael Dawson, retired colonel, U.S. Infantry: You urged me to write my story from memory and you would support me with military facts and statistics to make it authentic. That made the book possible.

Christian Frey, TV director, German History Channel: It was quite an elation for me when you had me narrate my work on your six-hour documentary *War of the Century*, shown in Germany and America, then telling me to get published.

Thank you Holly Bartlett Johnson, secretary of secretaries.

I wrote this work not for profit but for those loved ones who seek knowledge and understanding of a most violent and emotional happening. I hope this helps.

CONTENTS

Photographs from Camp Wheeler,
the Basic Infantry Training Center in Macon, Georgia. March 1943.

INTRODUCTION

What follows is a personal account of infantry combat in a far-away time and place. Far away but yet not so far, since human values and emotions transcend time and space. It is a young man's story written by the same man now not so young. It is also true that while young men go to war, a part of them ages in those forever moments where death and eternity seem very close. The images of war linger and remain as starkly terrible as they were in 1944. They can also provide lessons for us all.

I wore my army-green colonel's uniform to Rotary lunch one day and I met Bill Meller. Looking for a place to sit down, he looked at my Combat Infantryman's Badge and said, "I've got one of those." Registering his age, I asked, "Europe or Pacific?" He replied, "Europe," and since I'd spent almost eight years of Cold War service in Germany, I asked him where. "Oh, a place you never heard of," he answered. "A town called Schmidt."

Bill and I both led infantry platoons in combat. My war was in the Republic of Vietnam, and on a relative scale, I was trained. Afterward, many of us who stayed in decided we would be better trained for the next one, and we began to look at examples from the past. Since Europe would be the most likely point of conflict, we looked hard at World War II. Battered copies of World War II histories were packed away in rucksacks and kitbags. Two examples we all studied at the Command and General Staff College were Schmidt and the Battle of the Bulge. Schmidt was a detailed example of what not to do against a professional and determined enemy, and the Bulge stands as an example of how to recover from surprise and defeat an enemy offensive.

Later in Europe, World War II maps in hand, I had my infantry battalion's officers walking the same trails that Bill walked. We looked out of their foxholes and we tried to learn from their sacrifice and example. As professionals with the minimum of a commission and the infantry school, we stood in the fog and rain in awe of what young men, hastily trained and unprepared, had done in those dark and hallowed forests along the German border. In the words of one 1944 infantryman, "We could look forward only to being killed, wounded, or captured."

It gave me great satisfaction to reply to Bill, "I've been to Schmidt, and I want to hear your story." I believe you will, too.

Michael T. Dawson
Colonel Infantry U.S. Army (Ret.)

Meller at U.S. Army Induction Center, New Cumberland, Pennsylvania.
February 25, 1943.

Infantry Basic Training Drill Instructors, from left:
Cpl. Ed Nelson, Pfc. Meller, Cpl. Gus Voss, Cpl. Andy Andrews,
with Lt. Dominick Spinnozi (right). Brothers of Phi Kappa Psi,
at Camp Maxey, Texas. July 1944.

COURTESY OF THE AUTHOR

Summer, Ligonier Valley, Pennsylvania

My family was on vacation, staying in a cottage in the Pennsylvania mountains. I was eleven years old, and I found a loaded BB gun. In the woods, I saw a robin in a tree. The gun went off almost by itself and the robin fell to the ground, dead. When I picked it up, I saw it was a female, a mother. I cried when I placed the bird in the little box, then dug a hole under the tree for burial. After the burial, I stood there with tears in my eyes and I swore I would never kill another living thing, ever. This secret has stayed with me, that I stole the life of this creature for no reason at all. I was too ashamed to tell anyone.

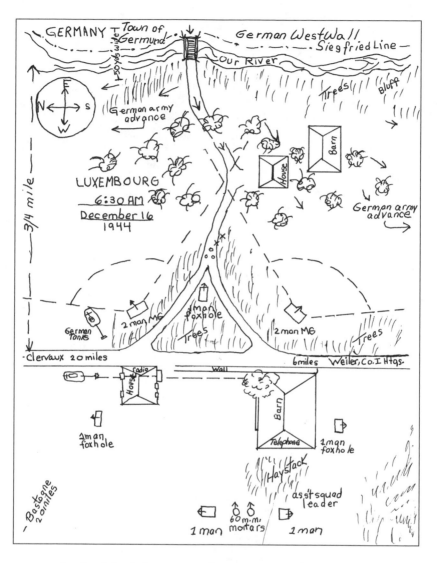

Battle of the Bulge outpost location, November 14, 1944,
through December 16, 1944.

2nd platoon, I Company 110th Regiment, 28th Division,
included S/Sgt. Meller and a platoon of eleven men.
This hand-drawn map shows the German-Luxembourg border
facing the German West Wall, Siegfried Line.

CHAPTER 1

The Battles

16 December 1944, 6:30 A.M.

My legs won't move; my feet are caught and I keep hearing these hideous screams. The head with no face is staring at me, a glistening white bone is pointing from the blood-soaked mess that was once someone's son, another son is crying for the mother that will never hear his voice again, a body is searching for its head, and the maddening fear that this insane anguish won't go away. I'm not a poor soul lost in this madhouse, but one of the healthiest, most intelligent, and strongest of our American youth. How did I get here? How do I get out?

The ring startles me. I'm soaked with sweat. Is it a dream? The frantic voice on the telephone whispers, "Sarge, the field in front of us is filled with krauts, hundreds of them, armed to the teeth. They don't see us. What'll we do?" This is no dream. I swallow.

"Open up with your machine gun, short bursts for the next five minutes, then fire only when you see something. Tell Red to fire his BAR. Synchronize your watch. It's six-thirty. I'll get back to you."

13

It's black as a pit outside. I don't know it, but it's the beginning of the Battle of the Bulge.

I think to myself, *This is must be a combat patrol looking for prisoners, and they're in our front yard. Our machine guns will scare the hell out of them and run them back to Germany.* I ring the foxhole on the left.

"Swing your machine gun around toward the road; we have visitors. You'll hear Colonel and Red firing. Short bursts for the next five minutes, then fire at will. It's six thirty-one."

The shaky voice croaks, "It's so damn foggy we can't see anything, where are they?"

"Remember, Bill is in the foxhole between you and Colonel. Watch your line of fire, I'll get back to you." Heading out the back door of the barn, I grab my assistant squad leader. "John, we're being attacked in the front along the road. Fire both mortars, ten shells each, rapid fire; then stop. Elevation over the barn, two hundred yards in front. Send one of your men to the right foxhole; tell Tex to slow fire his rifle into the fog, about two clips, then hold up." I head for the left foxhole.

Charlie asks, "What's all the noise, Sarge?"

"The Germans are attacking. We're trying to scare them off. Keep your eyes open; fire only if you see something."

"They're not over here yet."

"They will be."

"But, Sarge, I'm out here alone. I can't see anything in this fog."

"I know."

We are the 2nd Platoon, I Company, 110th Regiment, 28th Division, and we are alone. I'm the squad leader, recently promoted to staff sergeant, and I am not alone. We are twelve; we should be forty. I'm the ranking noncom; there is no platoon

14

leader. We're only 25 percent of our platoon strength. This is no time for a battle. It's up to me.

Two .30-caliber machine guns, two 60mm mortars, and seven rifles are making lots of noise. Fingers of dense fog are reaching out and grabbing us in this eerie predawn darkness. The Germans can't see our positions or us; they aren't close enough to see the house and barn in the dark and fog. They must be feeling our firepower by now, and they'll have no idea of our strength or weakness as long as the fog stays. It'll be light in another hour or so. We know where they were, but by now they'll be moving. The trick is to make them believe we are a much larger force. I learned in the Huertgen Forest battles that when we fire, we give it absolutely everything we've got. One thing we're not short of is ammunition. There's no tomorrow here, there's only now. I tell the men, "If we can't kill them, we will scare them to death."

No American troops are nearby to help us. The nearest help is I Company Headquarters, six miles south down this road at the little town of Weiler, and there is nothing in between. K Company is a good five miles to the north on this same road. We are placed in and around an old Luxembourg farmhouse and barn, three-quarters of a mile west of the German-Luxembourg border. The Our River is the natural border and behind that is the Siegfried Line. Bastogne is twenty-five miles behind us to the west and Battalion Headquarters is at Constun, fifteen miles behind us. We're defending a road junction, a macadam road that runs directly toward us from Germany. It dead-ends at our position, forming an inverted T with the road that runs parallel to the border. This road leads to Regimental Headquarters at the town of Clervaux, about twenty miles northwest, and behind us is nothing but space. In our front yard are the Germans, and it's us and them.

16 December 1944, 7:15 A.M.

We've been taking return fire from the Germans for an hour; small arms, burp guns, machine pistols, and rifles. There is no mistaking the sound. They are firing at the sound of our machine guns. Machine guns always attract fire. The high pitch of the German burp guns and machine pistols sounds like a dentist's drill grinding my teeth. It seems closer in the dark of night. God, I hate this sound. It's the sound of death. I make my way to the machine gun on the right, and in this dark I almost walk right by it. Small-arms fire from the Germans is coming from the southeast. They're probably waiting for daylight. Maybe they've turned around and gone home. I think to myself, *How many of them are out there?*

"We can't see anything in this soup, Sarge, I don't know where they are," says Red.

"Don't fire unless you see something. They aren't sure where we are," I say, "so be careful, they may be right out there in front of you. They can crawl right up to the edge of this foxhole before you'll see them. I'm going to check Bill." My adrenaline is up; I'm ready for this. I have learned how to fight.

16 December 1944, 7:30 A.M.

It's still dark and the fog is getting worse. The men are jumpy. This is their first taste of the enemy. Inching my way through the trees, I feel each tree like an old friend. I switch my carbine to my left shoulder and remove my Colt .45 from its holster. I cock the hammer and release the safety; it's ready to fire. The .45 is better for close contact in case I bump into one of them. It will blow off a head or dismember a body. Stopping, I listen for any sound. I can hear my heart thumping; the noise is loud. Krauts could be in these trees. They could hear me. I'm making too much noise breathing through my mouth. I try breathing through my nose. There is nothing but the sound of the Germans' small-arms fire; they must be going after Colonel's machine gun. I can't hear it. The softness of the earth quiets my steps for the twenty yards I've covered. I might bump into the enemy; it's just as dark for the Germans as it is for me. They are around here some-where; where the hell are they? I feel like screaming, *Here I am.*

Now I feel the macadam road under me, and I'm closer to the foxhole. It should be on the other side of this road. This is like being blindfolded. The ground goes upward.

I've found the foxhole. I don't want the Germans to hear me. I'm down on my knees. I whisper, "Bill, it's Sarge." It's as quiet as a tomb. I don't want him to shoot me. He may not recognize me in this fog. Leaning over the hole, I see him. He's dead, lying on his stomach at the bottom, my most trusted man. He had just returned from the hospital yesterday. The back of his jacket is covered with those little black shrapnel pieces from the German grenade. His helmet is beside him, blown off. I turn him over. He is unmarked. His face is peaceful and clean. The spent German grenade is in the hole next to him. The concussion killed him instantly. There's no ammunition clip in his rifle. He must have been loading his piece when it happened. I shouldn't have sent him out here. I feel sorrow; I am so sorry. Tears blur my eyes; I feel a terrible hatred for the son of a bitch who killed him. I hate all Germans. If it weren't for the Germans, we wouldn't be here. Bill wouldn't be dead in this dirty hole in the ground; he would be home in Georgia, where he belongs. I hear the German small-arms fire just past those trees.

I position Bill's body so it looks like he's watching the road and the machine-gun emplacements to the left and the right. He will be okay until this is over. This foxhole is in the center, where the road splits into an inverted V before it meets the dead end, thirty yards in front of the house and barn. This spot is heavily wooded and in daylight this position has a field of fire straight down the road for a half mile. A quarter mile farther down the road is the Our River, the Siegfried Line, and the German Army. I don't have an extra man to replace Bill, but I will come back and get him when this is all over. I pick up his rifle and ammunition and head for the foxhole on the left. My heart is heavy, but I can't show my remorse in front of the troops; they all will have so much to carry now.

This position is thirty yards to the left and north of Bill's foxhole. These three positions form a semicircle. Like the machine-gun emplacement to the right, this one is manned by two soldiers, the machine gunner and an ammunition carrier, both with M1 rifles and grenades. I stumble against a tree. I see them. "Bill just got it with a grenade. That means the German was close enough to see him or to see his rifle fire. Be very careful the krauts don't do the same thing to you. You didn't hear or see me approaching until I identified myself. I could have blown you away."

"This is our first time in combat and we haven't seen a kraut yet. We fired short bursts for five minutes into thin air. This fog is like mush. We didn't even hear you coming up on us. We may end up shooting each other."

I have to agree with him. "Keep your eyes open, I'm going to check Pete."

Next is the foxhole to the north, closer to the house. I iden-tify myself and ask if any krauts are in sight.

"I haven't seen anything out there in the dark. I heard the fire from both sides earlier, but it's quiet now. What are those krauts over there shooting at?"

"Us."

"Did anybody get hit?"

"Yeah, Bill got it with a grenade; they snuck up on him."

"Jesus."

"Don't fire until you see something and . . . be careful. I'm going to the house.

"Take those grenades off your jacket and lay them in front of you," I whisper. "You'll be needing them soon."

Holstering the .45, I remove the carbine from my shoulder and release the safety, and slowly pick my way through the fog.

At the back of the barn, my assistant squad leader, John, and the mortar crew greet me. John and I escaped through the Ger-man lines together in the Huertgen Forest, just last month.

"We deepened the holes just in case," he reports. "Why don't we disperse twenty more mortars out front five hundred yards just to keep them away from here?"

I smile. "Good idea, slow fire this time." I'm beginning to like my new assistant squad leader. This is the first time I've smiled all morning. John is about my age, a likable gentleperson with a round face, wearing glasses. I silently hope he stays around.

I tell him, "Bill got it in front of the house."

"How?"

"A grenade."

"God, I'm sorry. I know you liked him."

"Yeah," I say slowly. "There are only eleven of us now; we have to be very careful. If the krauts come in this way, open up;

I'll hear you. I'm going to the house and try the radio; give me one of your men."

"Take Slim."

Slim goes to work on the radio in the kitchen. He speaks to Company Headquarters, and a lone voice tells him no one is there, everyone is outside fighting the Germans. He calls Battalion, no answer; he calls Company again, no answer.

"Okay, open it up and use Mayday. We need tank support right now," I order.

After a while he sounds like a broken record.

"Mayday, Mayday, this is Fox 2, we need tank support right now, come in, come in."

I can hear the mortars doing their dirty work and I also hear return fire from the Germans, all small arms. It's good they aren't throwing heavy stuff. They could put us out of business. I sure hope the crew hits something with those mortars.

Slim looks up from the radio. "Are those our mortars?"

"Slim, keep on the radio and stay in here out of trouble."

----

16 December 1944, 7:45 A.M.

I swing through the barn and get Colonel on the field phone.

"We're holding our fire until we see something," he reports.

"How far can you see down the road to Germany?"

"We can't even see the road, visibility is about fifteen feet. We're afraid they'll sneak up on us like they did Bill."

"Keep your grenades in front of you," I warn him. "Use them only if you think you hear something. We can't afford any more casualties."

"Thanks," he mutters.

I reach into the big thermos and pull out some pancakes, then spread them with strawberry jam and wrap them around some bacon. Man, are they good. I didn't know I was hungry. So far, the Germans haven't jumped us. I better check around outside again. I head out back to the mortar crew.

---

16 December 1944, 8:00 A.M.

I grab the two remaining mortarmen and head back out front. "I want to see if we can find anything in this fog. Follow me." We walk slowly and very carefully through this soup. John's mortars are making a racket, and the shells are falling in front of us, to our right. I feel good. This is the first time I've heard mortars that weren't coming at me. I've never been on the defense before. Dawn provides some light, but the fog reduces visibility to about ten feet. I can reach out and touch the fog. This is dangerous as hell. We walk past the foxhole where Bill lies and both men see the body of their dead comrade. No one says anything. They don't have to; the body says it all.

I am surprised at my calmness; it feels good. I seem to be in complete control; I know exactly what I am to do. The mortars have stopped. It's deathly quiet, like a graveyard. Each adversary is waiting for the other to show himself, like a chess game. There is no sound whatsoever. What the hell is out there in this fog? Those bastards could be right in front of us. I look down and see the black macadam road underneath me; the snow is melting. We could be walking right into a German machine gun; we have before. Our rifles are at the hip, loaded and unlocked. We are ready to blast anything that comes out of the fog. I'm in front with the other two slightly behind, on my right and left. We are walking quietly and very slowly on the macadam road away from the ill-fated foxhole.

I don't want to get out here too far, my machine gunners don't know we are on this road. Our mortars are talking again, falling to the right ahead of us. The German fire is spasmodic, as if they're moving away to our right front. I think, *Maybe it is a patrol and they're leaving.* I don't want to walk out here too far and get hit by my own men. We aren't making a sound. The quiet is maddening. How much farther can I afford to walk? I don't want to get lost in this fog. My mouth is dry and I'm edgy, waiting for something to happen.

My heart jumps, I'm so startled. I almost bump into them. There are two of them in gray uniforms, a captain and a medic. They are right in front of me. I have never been this close to two live-armed German soldiers. They've walked right out of the fog into my arms. I wave my hands up. It's in their eyes; they know how close they came to being shot.

The medic raises his hands. The captain is wounded in the right arm. He is staring right into my eyes as he raises his left arm. I am staring at him. He wants to say, *Don't kill me.* He remains quiet and continues to stare. The medic has a pistol in his belt, a Luger. I motion for it and he hands it to me. I relieve the captain of his P38 Walther and stick both guns into my belt. The captain is young and clean-cut; the medic is older and grungy looking, wearing a steel helmet and the Red Cross armband. All this time my two companions are pointing their raised rifles at the two Germans, ready to fire.

"Let's shoot them," says one GI.

I hold up an arm and say, "We're not murderers, we're not going to shoot them."

"The medic is carrying a weapon; that violates the Geneva Convention. We can shoot them."

I turn to him and say, "What the hell do you know about the Geneva Convention? You shoot them and I'll blow your fuckin' head off." I remember him; he was inducted into the Army right out of federal prison. He's one of my great new replacements. All three of them had been prison inmates the day they were inducted into the Army. I was stuck with them.

"You two take the medic."

"What do we do with him?"

"Head for the barn and keep your eyes open; there may be more of them."

The captain's eyes are on me as I nod and point my rifle down the road. He follows the two GIs and I follow him. He is my size, five foot ten, 175 pounds, and about my age, twenty years. I can't wait to speak with him. He must know what this is all about. Why are all these German soldiers here? What's the purpose of all this? What has happened to our telephone and radio communication?

I keep my rifle in the captain's back as I look left and right for more Germans. A bunch could be hidden in this fog. They can blow us away in seconds. I feel uneasy. This happened so fast, it was almost too easy. If they had had their guns in their hands as we did, we might be the ones with our hands up. But they didn't. I wonder why. We are now within the semicircle of the gun emplacements and inside our line of fire. I'm surprised how calm I am. The Germans must be all around us, but we found only two. So far, there are no more casualties. I can't afford any more.

I walk our prisoners slowly down the road toward the house, stop at the foxhole, and point to Bill's dead body. Both Germans understand.

"Tell John to meet me in the house, and you stay with the mortars," I tell the loudmouth GI.

"Yeah," he grunts.

To the other one I say, "You take the medic into the barn and stay with him, if he moves, shoot him; if he escapes, I'll shoot you. I'll take the captain into the house."

I say to the other, "I don't want the medic and the captain together."

We enter the house and I say to the radioman, "Get off that thing for a while and see what you can do with this German's wound."

"I know what to do."

I give John the medic's Luger. "A souvenir for you. One of your mortar shells nicked the captain."

"We fired twenty shells, there're only a few left. We can't see the results in this fog. We'd better hold on to what we have, we don't know what's going to happen next."

"Okay, we don't get anything on the radio; we seem to be isolated. I'm going for a walk to see what's on the other side of that ridge. Stay with the captain until I get back. I don't know why it's so quiet out there."

I visit the foxhole to the north, left of the house. "Meller here."

"I hear you. I haven't seen a thing, haven't fired my rifle since early this morning. What's going on?"

I bring him up-to-date and tell him to come into the barn for some pancakes and coffee that were brought in last night for our breakfast. Company sends the food by jeep late in the afternoon. They bring hot food in large thermos containers, the day's dinner and the following morning's breakfast. We have bacon, pancakes, strawberry jam, and coffee for breakfast.

"I'll wait here for you," I say. "When you finish, tell Mike and Joe to come in." When a man comes in for his food, he won't take as much time when there is no one to talk with. One by one, each man is relieved and fed in a short time. After he eats, he returns to the foxhole. I don't need a committee meeting this morning.

I walk through the barn. The GI and the German medic are snug. "I'm depending on you to keep him here," I say. He nods in agreement. I walk across the road from the barn toward the right foxhole, facing southeast. I can see a little better in this fog now, as the dark of night is gone. I arrive at the foxhole.

"Those mortars came down out there all over the place. It's too foggy to see if they caused any damage," Red reports.

"It's nice that they were our mortars for a change."

I brought him up-to-date on our two prisoners. "That's great, maybe we can trade those two krauts for a ticket out of here." Little did we know how true these words would turn out to be.

-----

16 December 1944, 10:00 A.M.

"Red, keep your eye on me. I'm going to walk over that ridge to see if there's anything out there. If you see anything, cover me." This is hairy and I have no idea what's over there, but the Germans have to be somewhere. Where the hell did they all go? The two we captured walked right into our arms, and they were headed somewhere. Not a word on the radio from anywhere; it's like everyone dropped off the end of the earth.

I'm carrying my M1 carbine, and the Colt .45 is on my hip. I confiscated both of these from dead American soldiers. The carbine clips are fastened to the stock of the M1, the .45 magazines are on my belt, two grenades hang from each of my two jacket pockets, and my combat knife is in my right boot.

A slight ridge is about fifty yards ahead of me. The pines smell good in this crisp cold air, like lots of Christmas trees. I wonder if I'll see one this year. A slight breeze is swirling the fog. I can see about fifty feet; this is better. It's getting much lighter, although the overcast is low in the sky. The snow has vanished with the warmer temperature. It must be about thirty-three degrees. I've got to be careful I don't get shot; there may be German snipers anywhere and we don't have a medic. Nothing is visible. I'm thinking, *It is as quiet as a graveyard.* I come out of the wooded area and stop under a tree. What I see paralyzes my senses. I try to swallow, but my mouth is too dry. I am damn near in shock. How did I get into this? There isn't much fog out in front of me; never have I seen anything like this. A shallow valley is below me. It's a pastureland about a mile away, with no fog at all.

From here, the valley looks to be about three miles wide. The valley is completely filled with German troops. This is no combat patrol; this is an invasion. Everything imaginable that makes up an army is in front of me: armored infantry, personnel carriers, self-propelled artillery, jeeplike vehicles, antitank guns, and thousands of foot soldiers. They are spread out as far as I can see. Bunched up, they look as if they have no fear of air or artillery attack. This looks like a full division. (After the war, I learned that I was looking at the 130th Panzer-Lehr division.) I am glad they're over there and not here. They would run over us and not even hear us scream. They must have crossed the Our River at the new wooden bridge, then dispersed on a wide front. I had continually requested that the company commander have this bridge blown. It's still there and obviously the Germans are using it; our machine-gun and mortar fire must be keeping them from using this road. And with the fog hiding our position, they must have found it faster to go around us than to fight. They are smart.

Next, they'll want possession of this road junction, and we are sitting right smack on top of it. Sooner or later the shit is going to hit the fan. No American troops are in the valley, and Company I Headquarters is three miles beyond the valley. We are stuck. Small wonder we couldn't make radio contact with Company or Battalion. This is a bad deal. We may have to leave our positions and fight our way out of this.

I walk slowly back to the machine-gun foxhole. "We have more company than we need, just over that hill. Take a look. For now, the krauts are heading away from us on this side."

Colonel climbs out of the hole to stretch. "You mean we are surrounded?"

"Yep."

"Shit, I wanted to be home for Christmas."

"We'll have to move these krauts out of here first."

I head back to the farmhouse. I am beginning to sag.

---

16 December 1944, 11:00 A.M.

Slim and the German captain are getting along fine. "I treated his arm and bandaged it; the sling should make him more comfortable," reports Slim. "It's a slight wound the German medic fixed."

I nod to the German and we walk, in single file, into the front room of the house. We both sit in chairs. He says he speaks some English. "Thank you for the food and for attending to my wound, also for not shooting the medic and me." We are sizing up each other. "Are you in charge here?" he asks. I nod. He must be thinking, *How could this simple dogface and his troops have turned back our assault with such an insignificant force?* I'm thinking, *Where is he headed and what part does he play in all of this?* He is dressed in an impeccable gray dress uniform, black boots, and a field officer's cap. He carries a binocular case and a beautiful leather map case slung over his shoulders. I'm dressed in a worn field jacket, dirty, worn pants, and beat-up combat boots. On my head is a steel helmet. He is dressed for a parade, while I look ready to mop the floor.

He is about my age, a captain with the Iron Cross at his throat and the decoration for the Battle of Stalingrad on his tunic. These are two very commendable decorations.

He is a good-looking blond man, probably athletic. The girls in Germany, or anywhere, would find him an attractive male. He seems intelligent, and I'm gaining respect for him.

"I wish to repay your kindness by saving your life and those of your men. You have done a commendable job here." As he speaks, I relieve him of the map case. In this discussion, I am the one with the gun and he is the one without. His map case is of shiny, new, quality leather. I open it, and my eyes pop. The first map is a drawing of our position. Machine-gun emplacements are in red, mortars in green, and foxholes with riflemen in black. The farmhouse and the barn are drawn to scale, even the haystack. When he walked out of the fog into my arms, he knew exactly where he was supposed to be and just exactly how many men we had. This shakes me, but I smile and say, "Well done." He nods in return.

"There are three hundred companies of three hundred men each, coming down this road. They will take this position. Surrender now and save your life and those of your men." He describes the killing of both German and Russian troops at Stalingrad and the Russian front. As he speaks, it dawns on me how the Germans obtained this information shown on this map.

I smile and say, "The farmhouse." He just looks at me, as if to acknowledge. Well, I'll be damned. The other farmhouse and barn are located straight down the macadam road toward Germany. They sit on the right side of this road a half mile in front of our position. They are in plain sight. This area has wide-open pasture on all sides and the Our River is about a quarter mile due east on the road. The German Army is located on the far side of the river inside the Siegfried Line. A number of times, a few of us have stood in the woods overlooking the river, admiring the new bridge, listening to the Panther tanks charging their batteries, and watching the Germans in the chow line. It was weird being in a noncombat area, where neither side was killing the other. This was a rest area for the soldiers of both armies. At least, it was until this morning.

Mid-November 1944

Every other day, just before daybreak, I took three men and went out to the farmhouse. There, by order from the company commander, we observed the area between the house and the river. We expected the Germans would send over patrols, either to observe us or take prisoners for interrogation. This was expected, as we routinely did the same thing. Last week an American night patrol stopped in to see me to check their location. They had been sent from Battalion Headquarters to report on German positions. When we spotted a German patrol, we went after them. Either they would get us or we would get them, often some of both.

I was frustrated with my superiors. My many requests for booby traps and land mines were totally ignored. Since the three GIs with me were ex-convicts, I thought they might have an idea how we could protect ourselves from surprises from the Germans. Every day that we didn't visit the farmhouse, the Germans were free to do so. I didn't want to walk into that house and get blown away. Our ad hoc committee decided on hand grenades, with the pin removed and the handle held down with piano wire. We placed the grenades in a large ceramic pot in the hallway and ran the piano wire across the floor to the kitchen entrance.

The wire was about two inches off the floor and anything, man or beast, that passed through that doorway would trip it. The grenades would explode and carry all those ceramic and steel shrapnel pieces into the perpetrator. I wasn't proud of this weapon, but we had no better ideas for our security. As long as these booby traps remained in place, I would know the house had not been violated. It would be reasonably safe for us to enter. Throughout the daylight hours the men in the machine-gun emplacements kept their eyes on the house. We didn't see anything at night; it was black as sin.

The next day went by without any explosions, and nothing was heard during the night. The following morning we arrived at the house on schedule without any surprises from the Germans, or so we thought. We always approached the house just before daybreak, using darkness as our cover. We waited until first light, then entered the house. We searched the house, room by room, then the barn. I had recently secured a Colt .45 automatic from the body of a dead officer; now I had something to enter the room with. The M1 rifle was awkward.

We cleared each room the same way. It was more than a little bit hairy. A GI stood on each side of the door; then I burst in with my heart in my mouth and the Colt .45 in front of me, something like Wyatt Earp at Dodge City. The two GIs followed me into the room, ready for whatever may be there. When we left at night, we kept all the doors open clearing the house and the barn. We then examined our security device, and were surprised. Both grenades were in their original posi-

tion, but the piano wire was wrapped around the grenade handles. The piano wire had been unfastened, there was no more trip wire; it was wrapped around the handles. There was no way the grenade could have exploded unless the wire was entirely unwrapped. Who did this? When?

Who did this was obvious. It wasn't any of us; it was the bad guys. When was it done? Anytime we were not here in the house. Spooky? It sure was. We just looked at one another. We could have been killed by our own booby trap. I felt the cold chill run down my back. We reset the device when we left again that night. The next morning when we arrived, the device was again dismantled. I had enough, I called it off. No more booby traps, we could all have been the victims. The Germans could have blown us all away. Why didn't they? I think it's because they would have lost their observation post—the observation post we thought was ours. I felt like an idiot. I was an idiot. We all were getting jumpy.

I told the company commander about this. "We need someone in that house twenty-four hours a day."

He didn't see it that way. "Just keep doing it the same way."

I had my own opinion. We had five weeks of this farmhouse duty and we saw only one German soldier. He was way off in the woods; in a second he was gone. The days we didn't inhabit the house, the Germans had the opportunity to observe us. With binoculars they could see all they wished, undeterred. They evidently had a better sense of humor than we did. If they had wanted to destroy us, they sure had the opportunity.

---

16 December 1944, 1:00 P.M.

The German observers' excellent work is illustrated on the map I have before me. Does the captain know how this all came about? I guess I'll never know. Our discussion is over; I thank him for his concern for my troops and me. I find myself liking him. The question is how to guard the captain and the medic. When the Germans decide to come after us, we will need every available man. I walk him to the barn and confine him and the medic in a closed room. The GI remains on guard.

Nothing from the radio; we decide to give it a rest. In the kitchen, I can see through the window that the fog is blowing away. I open the window. Through the binoculars, I can see across the bare fields to the horizon. The fog is almost gone. It must be half a mile north to the ridge that dips out of sight. There on the horizon are German troops walking along like stragglers. I automatically pick up Slim's M1 rifle. Again I look at the Germans, almost in a single line. I push up the rifle sight as far as it goes.

There is no need for windage. I lean the rifle on the windowsill and unlock the safety. While I qualified as an expert with the .45 and machine gun, I qualified only as marksman with the M1. In basic training we weren't shown the maximum range of this piece. Maybe it will shoot eight hundred yards. Now I will know. The sight is on the first German in line. I move it just in front of him to compensate for the distance. He will walk into the bullet, if it carries that far. I fire. He goes down and they all scatter out of sight. I think, *That will teach you krauts to stay away from us.*

Slim turned around. "Did you get him?"

"Yeah, those krauts will stay off that ridge now."

"The shooting has stopped, maybe they're taking a rest."

I didn't tell him what I had seen down in the valley. "Maybe," I answered. I head for the barn.

All my troops are fed and watered. The silence of this lull makes me uneasy. Combat troops need to be uneasy. They stay alert and often alive. They'll be coming after us; the only question is when. I sit down in my corner. The telephone and my sleeping bag are here. I'm glad I ran telephone wire to each of the three foxholes, it's worked out so far. Life here in Luxembourg has been so much better than in the Huertgen Forest. There we lived and fought in and around our foxhole. Living in a hole in the ground is filthy, cold, and wet; dying in it is even worse. Here it's clean, dry, and peaceful, at least it was until this began. We have all been able to sleep with our shoes off; that in itself has been a blessing. Wet, cold feet develop into trench foot, as many a sad GI has experienced. Trench foot often results in the amputation of the toes or the entire foot. Dry socks and foot circulation prevent trench foot by keeping the feet healthy, but life in the foxhole is both cold and wet.

I've been so happy here, it seems almost sinful. Two weeks ago, the company commander ordered me to headquarters. "You've earned a week's leave in Paris; enjoy it," he said. "This leave is awarded to the soldier in the line with the most longevity." Today, I wonder if the Germans understand that in two days, December 18, I'm leaving for Paris.

---

6 December 1944

Cleaning my Colt .45 I heard a voice say, "Are you in charge here?" I stood up, and lo and behold, there standing in front of me was a real live general. I thought, What the hell are you doing here in my barn?

"Yes, sir."

"Why aren't you wearing your bars?"

"I'm a staff sergeant, not an officer," I replied.

33

"Where is your platoon leader?"

"He's been court-martialed. The platoon sergeant and a private have been taken to the hospital. The platoon guide and another soldier are laid out in front of a German pill box over near the border."

"I am General Cota, your division commander," he said.

I told him the squad, which is supposed to be a platoon, is in position. He ignored that. General Cota was commander of the 28th Division, which had recently suffered over 6,500 casualties in the Huertgen Forest campaign. Although I participated, luckily I was not among the 6,500. The 28th was relieved, then transferred to this Luxembourg location for rest and regrouping with new replacements. We needed lots of replacements. We were positioned along this border with gaps of five or six miles between emplacements. The enemy could walk through our front line and we wouldn't know it. This was mighty scary. From mid-September through mid-December, some thirty-four thousand Americans, and probably as many Germans, were killed, wounded, captured, or evacuated with pneumonia, trench foot, and combat exhaustion. My comrades were gone. I was glad to be one of the few fortunates to remain. Good riddance to the Huertgen Forest.

The two of us walked outside, where we joined other ranking officers, who were standing around two command cars and a few jeeps. The jeeps held enlisted men and officers, and it looked like a small parade on Veterans Day. The general's vehicle had two little flags on the front fenders. I thought the krauts would like to see this, and I wondered if the general knew how close he was to the German Army. I decided not to remind him. We proceeded to the machine-gun and the mortar emplacements, then the foxholes I had originally arranged in the area. After complimenting me on the emplacements, he began his lecture on the rifleman in combat. It was his theory that this was a sergeant's war.

"The combat infantryman moves forward, firing his rifle at the enemy. When he falls, another moves into his place, always forward,

then another and another. It is the sergeants that lead and see that the forward progress is carried through to meet the objective." I was thinking, Where the hell are the officers during all this? His last words were, "This war will be won by the foot soldier."

With that, they all piled into their vehicles and were off. I had never seen a general close up before, and I was not impressed. Maybe he caught my drift and would send some replacements. We were sadly undermanned. I thought, What happens if the Germans decide to cross the river?

As we would soon learn, they sure did decide that.

---

16 December 1944, 3:00 P.M.

It's much too quiet outside, so I decide to make the rounds. John, my assistant squad leader, is behind the barn with Joe. They both look tight; it's nervous time. John and I walk around this huge fifteen-foot-tall haystack where the mortars are installed. We had decided to install them here out of sight so they would not be in the line of fire if we were attacked. "Are these all the shells you have?"

"We have fifteen mortar shells left," he tells me.

"We'll need them, and more, when the krauts decide to come back. We're in good shape with K rations; they won't help us with the krauts, but we won't go hungry. We have nothing on the radio. Slim has been at it all day. We are stuck here until we get some help. They're behind us."

John is receptive. He knows that I'm counting on him. He and I have combat experience from the Huertgen Forest. The remaining nine of this group are replacements with no experience.

35

Each has performed well since he arrived here. I'm particularly pleased with the response from Colonel and Red; they are natural soldiers. They're dependable and follow orders well. Some men rise to the occasion sooner than others do and some drag their feet. I am responsible for them and I want them to stay fit and alive. It's tough when one goes down. I never had the opportunity to make friends before; they were all gone before I knew them.

I describe to John what I observed this morning.

"Sounds like we are surrounded again, just like the Huertgen Forest," he says. "Maybe we can get out like we did before."

"I hope we don't have to try that again."

As I put my arms around both of them, I'm thinking, *Ten men are all I have left. We all have to depend on one another to stay alive. I have to remain strong so they all are strong for what's ahead. Thousands of Germans are out there; sooner or later they'll be coming after us, and my men are depending upon me.*

Something has changed in me. Deep down inside I'm beginning to like soldiering; I'm even better when the action starts.

Colonel and Red are wide-awake and alert at their machine-gun emplacement. "I took a look at what you saw this morning. They're still coming across that field. I wonder when they'll be heading this way. You'd think they'd want this road junction."

"They will. You have how many belts left for that machine gun?"

"Only two. Don't we have any in the barn?"

"No."

"I have my M1 here and Red has the BAR."

"I have eight clips of ammunition for the BAR and a bandolier for the rifle," says Red. "Any more in the house?"

"No, this is a rest area, remember?"

"Some rest," Red mutters. "We'll get back into it before this day is over."

I remind him, "No one was concerned about ammunition, just rest and build up to strength, to go off and fight somewhere else."

"We used three belts this morning; we must have hit a bunch of them. They must have cleared away the wounded and the dead by now. I kept the line of fire at about a foot off the ground so they couldn't crawl under it. John's mortar fire landed all over them. None of them got close enough to give us any trouble, but they sure got close enough to Bill."

"Yeah. We'll know when they arrive. I'm going to check the other machine gun." I move off through the thinning fog. When the fog is gone, things will get hot.

On the way to the second machine gun, I notice the fog is lighter and the breeze is blowing it around. The air smells good. "Pete, the fog isn't hiding us as well now. You two had better stay in your foxhole. We don't want to attract any more krauts."

"Anything on the radio about tank support?"

"Not a thing all day, but Slim is working on it."

"I've got two machine-gun belts, I gave Colonel two of mine. We do have one bandolier of M1 ammunition." I am thinking to myself, *We don't have much ammo for a fight.*

"I decided to leave Bill's body for Grave Registration. I hope we don't have any more."

"Amen to that. I heard you got a kraut at eight hundred yards."

"Yeah, I'm not proud of it, but it's one less German. I'm going to check the radio." As I walk toward the house I think, *One less German. I didn't have to shoot him; he wasn't bothering me. What difference does it make? His death won't win the war for us. I took a life.*

I'm beginning to feel remorse for a man I don't even know. I really don't like killing. It's not the first time I felt badly about a killing.

---

16 December 1944, 4:00 P.M.

The light is beginning to go; it will be dark soon. I want to fight them in the daylight. I don't like this: they know we are here. We must have killed a bunch of them this morning. Night fighting is bad. I wonder if we will all be here tomorrow. The two prisoners might be better held in the house. In the barn the GI is standing guard.

"Bring out the prisoners. I'll take them to the house; you come along."

"Right."

As we walk across the barnyard I hear our machine gun on the left. "Shit, they must be coming." Rifle fire is beginning from two of the foxholes. We rush the two Germans inside the house and push them into the back room next to the kitchen. When I look out the window, there is nothing to see and the firing has stopped.

"Keep an eye on those two krauts," I tell the GI.

In the kitchen I listen to Slim on the radio calling for tank support. I look out the window. It's getting darker and I hear no noise from either machine gun. I wonder, *Are they still alive out there?* My attention is taken by Slim on the radio. Then I hear it: it's a heavy motor; it must be a tank.

"Our tanks are coming," I yell at Slim. "They're here." Looking out the window, I see it.

Slim says, "That's not ours; see the cross on the side?"

Damn, he's right, no white star of an American tank. This is a monster machine with the longest cannon I have ever seen. It's a German tank parked on top of the machine-gun foxhole. My two men must be dead. There is another one behind it, pulling up to my left. Just then I hear the front door of the house blow off. The explosion sounds like a dynamite charge.

I look; the door is gone. I'll be damned if those assholes are coming through *my* front door. I imagine they are going to rush the front doorway. I am standing at the open window. I turn and look through the window straight at the lead tank. I am petrified. I can't move my feet. I watch the nose of the cannon as it slowly turns and it is now pointed straight at me. That bastard is looking right at me. He is going to shoot me. I'll be killed.

I yell, "Slim, hit the floor!" We both crawl into the far corner of the kitchen, away from the window, put our heads down, and wait for the explosion. *Boom*, then *swoosh!* We hear the explosion.

"It hit the barn!"

"Did you see that?"

"I think so, the damn shell came through the window, down the hall, through the front doorway, and hit the barn."

"Boy, he can shoot."

"Come on," I yell. "Upstairs!" We both crawl up the stairs, dragging our rifles, to the second floor to get away from that tank. I look out the second-story window facing east and the road to Germany.

"That son of a bitch can really shoot."

It is now completely dark. Our machine gun on the right is firing; nothing from the left. The German tank must have finished them. American .30-caliber machine-gun bullets bounce off a German Panther tank like peas from a child's peashooter.

39

Only a .105 howitzer can stop a German Panther tank. We can't see anything but flashes from the German small-arms fire. They are coming this time. They are all around in front of us. We both begin firing at the flashes, Slim with his rifle and me with my carbine.

Slim calls, "I'm out of cartridges."

"I will be," I say as I finish off the last three rounds. The German bullets are hitting the roof above our heads; now we see the machine-gun tracers. The tracer bullets are coming right toward us, in through the window. "They know where we are. Shit, let's go!" We hit the floor and bounce back down the stairs. I don't know where anyone else is. The clip is empty for my Colt .45. I don't remember firing it, but it's empty. The German P38 is in my left hand; the clip is full. I release the safety.

John comes through the front doorway.

"They set fire to the haystack so they could see us; we had to get out. The mortar shells are all gone. My two men are in the barn."

"Okay," I tell him. "Stay here in the hall on the floor; I'm taking these two krauts into the front room."

"I have only one clip for my rifle."

"Give me some of your hand grenades. Can we strip some machine-gun belts?"

"We already have, we're down to nothing," John tells me.

I push the two Germans into the front room, over in the front corner so they'll be out of the line of fire. I kick open the front window; it swings out facing the courtyard. "John, use your hand grenades when they rush the front doorway."

The noise outside has stopped; not one shot is heard. They must have got by Red and Colonel and now they are around the house. Those tanks on the other side have quit firing because they know German ground troops are on this side of the house. This is a break.

In the pitch black of the house, I can just barely see the outline of the two Germans on the floor. I can't see anything else. John is about eight feet from me around the corner in the hallway. I can't see him in this dark. The open window is about five feet in front of me. In my side pockets are hand grenades. I pull the last grenade that's hanging from my jacket breast pocket. The loaded German pistol is in my belt. I'm sweating. The tension is unbearable. They're closing in on us. I've got to kill them to stay alive.

Where are they? I'm afraid they might hear my breathing. My heart is pounding and I can't stop the noise. I am breathing, very slowly through my nose to be as quiet as possible. I want to hold my breath, but I can't. The two Germans are quiet. Now there's not a sound in the house or outside.

Then I hear it. There is a soft scraping sound of a German leather boot against the macadam road out front; the krauts are crawling in the gully on the road next to the stone wall. The wall gives them cover as they crawl toward the front of the house. I can't see them. Even in the daylight, the wall would hide them. They are sneaking up on us, but they don't realize I can hear them.

I stoop down and lean out the doorway. John is behind me in the hall. I still can't see him in this darkness. I can't risk speaking to him. I know where the wall ends, even though I can't see it. Macadam roads in Luxembourg are built just like the ones we have in America, with a hump in the center so the rain washes off the road into the side gully. At home, I was a fair softball pitcher.

I pull the grenade pin, pitch the grenade underhand around the corner of the wall onto the hump of the road. The grenade makes a noise as it hits the road. I can hear it as it bounces back down into the gully against the wall; just like with firecrackers on the Fourth of July, I can tell my degree of accuracy by the explosion. It makes a hell of a noise against that wall. It works, they scream, and I throw the second one, more screams. It works too.

I hurry back into the front room. The two Germans are still on the floor. John fires six shots with his rifle through the doorway. He is out of ammunition. The window is only five feet in front of me; I toss a grenade out the window. It doesn't explode. I can hear the scraping. This time the German is under the window. He must have crawled by the doorway without John seeing him. I expect a German potato masher to come through this window if I don't get him first. I pull the pin, release the handle of the second grenade, count, "One, two," then let it go.

Bam! It goes off just under the window. There is no noise. How could I miss him this close? Maybe he's dead. Now I see the light of the burning haystack from behind the barn; it throws some light into the barnyard. No Germans are in the barnyard that I can see. I can't risk sticking my head out the window. With a grenade in my right hand and the pin in my left, I realize I don't even remember taking it from my pocket.

There are Germans outside, talking. I don't know where they are, but they're out there somewhere. I release the handle and this time count to three then toss the grenade. It hits the windowsill and bounces back into the room. I leap on top of the two Germans.

The explosion is deafening in this small room. I think we are dead. But no, no one is dead. I examine myself. I have a small cut on my nose and another on my wrist. I check the two Germans;

they are fine. None of us is hurt. The room stinks with the putrid stench of gunpowder, but no one complains; we are alive. I must have kicked the grenade under the table and it took the force of the explosion. As I step on the broken wood, I give a prayer of thanks. We should be raw meat. The three of us, the two Germans and an American, are three human beings, two soldiers trained to kill each other and one medic trained to keep us alive while we do it, and here we are helping each other survive. I am killing the Germans outside the house while I am protecting the ones on the inside. Does this make any sense? The grenades are gone; I have nothing left.

I hear the Germans telling us in English to come out with our hands over our head and no weapons. The Germans have illuminated the barnyard with lights much like a night baseball park. The GIs from the foxholes and the barn are already out there. Since all firing has stopped, I go back to the kitchen to discard the German pistol. There is a well-known rumor in the American Army: do not be captured with a German weapon, you will be shot on sight. I say a silent good-bye to the pistol as it sails out the back window.

The German weapon is better than our Colt .45 I carry. I remove the .45 from the holster and lay it on the table; it's empty, now I'm naked. I have no ammunition; none of us has any ammunition. We began firing at the Germans at 6:30 A.M., and now it's 7:00 P.M. Mortar-shell cases, machine-gun ammunition belts, BAR, and M1 rifle and carbine clips are all empty and gone. The hand grenades that kept us in business are all gone. Some of the krauts are all gone or going. And the saddest of all, Bill is gone. This has been hopeless and now we are helpless. I feel broken, God help me, I tried.

I think to myself, standing in the kitchen, that in the movies the good guys are rescued at the last minute. The tanks we heard this afternoon—we thought they were just what we radioed for. We had called for help all day and no one answered us. Instead, the tanks we saw were the bad guys. I can't believe this is the end. I don't want to walk out that door. There must be something I can do, something I haven't thought of. Even if we could kill all the Germans standing outside, there are more and more behind them. And we don't have anything left to kill them with. I still haven't figured a way out of this mess.

I reluctantly walk through the house and out the front door. The bright light blinds me. I'm the last one out. A German soldier points and I join my men at the front of the house. Everyone is there. No one has been wounded or killed. There are eleven of us in American uniforms standing in a straight line facing a German officer. Behind him are his staff officers and some nasty-looking soldiers with machine pistols pointed at us; farther back, I imagine, is the German Army. Shit.

Now I realize what is standing in front of me. He is something to behold, right out of a war movie. But this is no movie. He is obviously a general, wearing a long black leather coat with a fur collar and shoulder pads loaded with red and gold. He wears a monocle and carries a baton; his uniform and shiny boots are spotless. He is something to see and he scares the shit out of me.

The German soldier searches me and raises hell when he pulls the knife from my boot. Slim, next to me, speaks to him in German, then turns to me. "I told him you are the sergeant-in-charge. You saved the captain's life, dressed his wound, and fed him."

The general turns and begins yelling at the officers standing behind him. The GI next to me says, "The general is giving them hell for allowing eleven American soldiers to hold this road junction all day. We should have been wiped out first thing this morning. He wants to know why the Americans have no casualties. He tells them to count the dead and wounded German soldiers lying here."

This is happening so fast I can't even swallow. We all stand there, stiff, looking at those machine pistols. We are afraid to blink an eye. I have one thought that helps me gain a little courage. I'm getting pissed off that these assholes are scaring the pants right off me. If we'd had more ammunition, we could have blown away more of them. I am thinking the smart move this morning would have been to take off out the back door. Actually, the fog was so dense we couldn't have gone anywhere. This is frustrating, and I'm scared. These guys look as if they can't make up their minds whether to shoot us or not.

Now I see the German captain—my captain—pointing toward me as he speaks to the general. He wears the bloodstain on his uniform and his arm is still in the sling. I hope he remembers how I protected him from that exploding grenade. The uglies remain standing there with those machine pistols. No one has told them to leave. The thought hits me that they are going to execute us with the machine pistols. They can't do this, not after what we have just been through.

They don't.

As the general turns around and walks away, another officer speaks to us in English. "You will walk in single file with the German guards. You will not talk or make any sound. When you reach your destination, you will be counted. If anyone is missing, you all will be shot immediately."

45

We believe him. He adds, "The German Army has penetrated the American lines to a depth of thirty miles today and thousands of Americans have been captured."

We don't believe this, but none of us open our mouths. I'm beginning to wonder about just how many of my squad speak and understand the German language; how many were born in Germany? This is a bit frightening. Just who is us and who is them? We are permitted to leave with the clothes on our back, our helmets and canteens. This is better than the alternative. And so it draws to a close, this first day of battle of what would later be named "the Battle of the Bulge."

Report of Operations 16-18 December 1944, H. E. Fuller, Colonel, Infantry:

Over 2,100 Germans were buried in the 28th Division's 110th Regiment sector, covering the 10 1/2 mile front line from Heinerscheid [N] to Reisdorf [S].

The entire German 130th Panzer-Lehr division hit us straight on.

The American tanks, with ammunition, answering our call and coming to our aid, were turned back by the German advance, just behind us at the Red Ball highway.

Telephone lines had been cut by the enemy and radio communication was disrupted prior to the attack.

110th Infantry Regiment lost 2750 men, 48 tanks, and 8 artillery pieces.

In the afternoon, German tanks crossed the newly constructed wooden Our River Bridge to capture our road junction.

This three-day delay of the 2nd Panzer, 116th Panzer, and Panzer-Lehr saved Bastogne.

CHAPTER 2

Name, Rank, and Serial Number

16 December 1944, 8:00 P.M.

The night is as black as the inside of my pocket. I see only the man in front of me and the German soldiers passing close by. We all are deep in thought. I'm sure the Germans are having theirs. My stomach is empty; I last ate at seven o'clock this morning. I'm not hungry, not thirsty, but I am apprehensive. The Germans can walk us back here and shoot us. I know on good authority that the 28th Division insignia was called "the Bloody Bucket" by the Germans because of its reputation for shooting German prisoners. I wonder if these Germans heard the same thing.

Mid-October 1944, Huertgen Forest

We were moving through the woods up to the front line. Four GIs had passed us, taking a few captured Germans back to the rear.

The veteran soldier next to me had said, "They won't be gone long."

I didn't know what he meant. About twenty minutes later, the same GIs caught up with us, walking in the same direction as we were. They didn't have the Germans with them. The man next to me had said to one of the soldiers, "That didn't take long."

"Nope."

I had said to my companion, "Isn't it a mile back to headquarters?"

"Yep."

We begin to walk down the road in single file. As we walk by the farmhouse, I remember the chicken dinners there. One of the ex-cons was a burly fellow with a gigantic mustache. His story was that when home on leave in Chicago, although a private, he would dress as a colonel. In civilian life, he had been a steel rigger working high up on skyscrapers, and was well paid. On leave, he had been taking in the opera in his colonel's uniform that night with his entire family when the Military Police asked him for his identification. It wasn't long before he was out of his colonel's uniform and into the slammer. Naturally, we called him "Colonel."

---

18 November 1944, Luxembourg

Our first visit to the farm, Colonel found chickens in the barn. He also found corn and water and a chicken coop. So it began; on each visit to the farmhouse, Colonel cooked and we ate boiled chicken and boiled potatoes. Since we weren't exactly overfed on GI chow, this was a luxury. Things were quiet at the farm until one day we had visitors.

A jeep had just turned into our barnyard. I told my two men to stay put while I walked out to greet the new arrivals. There were two GIs, a major, and a captain in their nice clean uniforms. I stood in the path of the jeep and held up my hand for them to stop. In my Army fatigue jacket, I showed no stripes or insignia of any kind.

"*This area is off-limits,*" *I said.*

The major stood up in the jeep. "We're out looking for chickens to take back to Regimental Headquarters. I am the regimental supply officer."

"*This area is off-limits,*" *I repeated, and pulled out my Colt .45.*

"*Give me your name, rank, and serial number.*"

"*This is a combat zone, we don't give out information.*"

"*I am a major and we are coming in.*"

I told him as I cocked my gun, "If you put one foot on the ground, I am going to shoot out all the tires and you can walk all the way back to head-quarters. I'm a lousy shot and I might miss the tires and hit one of you."

So much for the chicken thieves.

This was great. A supply officer wouldn't have experienced any combat and he probably had never been on the wrong end of a gun before. I felt like I was doing this for every enlisted man in the Army. It felt good, just like at Tombstone. With that, the jeep turned around and they left. The major yelled, "I'm reporting you to the regimental commander."

As I turned back toward the house, I saw my two brave ex-con soldiers standing by the structure with their rifles ready, backing me up. I wondered if they would have used them. They had grins on their faces; I was their hero. They thought that I was one of the bad guys, just like them. Maybe I was. I felt great. All three of us had a better under-standing of each other.

"*The chicken's ready.*"

---

23 November 1944

The first time I saw the three of them was the day the Company I first sergeant handed them over to me at Company I Headquarters. He said,

"These are your replacements, more on the way. Two are from prison and one from the Army stockade."

I didn't say a word during the six-mile jeep ride back to the emplacement. When we arrived, I told them to follow me into the barn.

I liked the barn. It was large, roomy, clean, and it was quiet. It was my home and my office, although I'd never lived in a barn before. Everything was orderly and in place, the weapons, the food, and the manpower. The platoon leader, a first lieutenant, had taken the bedroom in the farmhouse. The platoon sergeant and the platoon guide, both technical sergeants, bunked there also. Since all three outranked me and I'd just arrived, I chose the solitude of the barn, where the men in my squad slept. I thought if anything happened, I would be close to my men. There was a good chance that if the Germans threw artillery in here, they'd go after the house first. The barn should be safer. My assistant squad leader was also close by. Never in my wildest imagination had I dreamed that the three in the house would be gone and I would be the ranking soldier here.

There was no one else in the barn, which was fine for my purpose. I looked at my three ex-cons, and told them that I was a squad leader only because eleven of our twelve-man squad had been killed, wounded, or captured in the Huertgen Forest campaign.

I told them, "Three of us promised a German soldier he would go to prisoner-of-war camp in America if he showed us how to get through the German lines and back to our own lines. He did. I'm the squad leader. If any or all of you give me any trouble or don't obey a command, I won't ask why, I'll shoot you in the back."

They became good soldiers and were always dependable. I was sorry to soon be parted from them.

16 December 1944, 9:00 P.M.

It's getting colder as we continue to walk quietly on the road past the farmhouse. I had walked this road with my weapons many times, and I never dreamed I would be walking it for the last time as a prisoner of war. I hope someone feeds the chickens.

We are now passing German troops. There are foot soldiers, tanks, armored carriers, half-tracks, command cars, automobiles, antitank carriers, 88 artillery pieces, and soldiers on bicycles and motorcycles. About half of the vehicles are horse-drawn; they seem to be low on gasoline. I am personally familiar with most of these weapons. At least I know what it feels to be on the receiving end of that firepower. The Germans have effective weapons, some superior to ours. Now and then the soldiers would say, "Russki." Maybe they think they're in Russia. Evidently the German assault was very secretive. I remember that the German captain wore the Battle of Stalingrad medal. Perhaps these troops had come from the Russian front. I'm not going to ask them.

A number of the soldiers wear a square-looking flashlight with red, green, and blue lenses on their uniform. They must use these to communicate silently in the black of night. These must be what caused the strange lights I saw in the Huertgen Forest— it sure looked spooky. I wonder why we Americans don't use this. It sure works for the Germans.

Early October 1944, Huertgen Forest

I had just finished my first twenty-four hours in a combat area. It was the Huertgen Forest. We had come in to the front line the day before, replacing the 9th Division. Each rifleman was assigned a foxhole vacated by the men we replaced. We were instructed to lay out our hand grenades and our rifle ammunition clips on the top of the foxhole, facing the enemy. It looked to me like this was what we were trained for: killing.

During the night, we took rifle and machine-gun fire from the Germans across from us in the woods. They had the nasty habit of sneaking in between our foxholes and getting behind us. I could see little lights off in the distance; the lights were moving around.

They were spooky. Then it began. It sounded like a charge. I'd never been in a charge. I'd never been shot at before either. I stood up and fired my rifle as fast as I could. I couldn't see any Germans, or anything else for that matter; it was too dark. I was scared. I just kept firing. The German fire was coming from the front and both sides. How can they do that? One advantage we had was that the M1 rifle, being semiautomatic, fired just as often as we could pull the trigger, while the German rifle was bolt action and much slower.

German soldiers did have one nasty weapon that we didn't have: a machine pistol that was completely automatic. This weapon made a high-pitched sound and was a good thing to stay away from. I didn't hear any noise from the foxhole on my right; the solider must have been hiding in it. I cursed him for being a coward. He couldn't be any more scared than I was. Any number of Germans could sneak right up by his hole and get both of us.

There wouldn't be any sleep that night. I wondered, Will I ever get any sleep? It was dead quiet; the firing had stopped. It just occurred to me, what the hell was I doing standing up? I could be killed. There was no one to talk to. I was alone again. The enemy was about one hundred yards into the woods across from me; I wondered if I would ever sleep with them this close. I was tired of being scared. I was getting colder; my feet were still cold, my socks were soggy, and my nose was running. It was a hell of a mess.

Somehow the morning finally came. A medic in the next foxhole bandaged the GI's hand, then led him away. He had shot off his thumb so he could be hospitalized. Did he know a self-inflicted wound means court-martial and a dishonorable discharge? He was gone and there was no one to fill that hole. What a rotten way to begin.

I found a .50-caliber machine gun and the ammunition belts in the foxhole. This was the gun used by our combat aircraft and tanks. I then laid them on top of my foxhole. I found a box of cartridge belts. I was all set for the night and whatever it would bring. The .50-caliber machine gun was an awesome weapon compared to the smaller .30-caliber rifle that I carried.

I was very nervous. Looking straight ahead in that black ink was weird. I had put my finger on the end of my nose and I couldn't see my finger. I didn't know it could be so dark. After a while I began to see things that probably weren't there. I remembered a movie, way back when I was small, called The Lost Patrol. *The French Foreign Legionnaires were holding an oasis in the desert from the Arabs. It was night and the Arabs were picking off the Legionnaires one by one by the light of the moon. Victor McLaglen was the one remaining soldier and he went completely nuts before they got him. What drove him batty was the fact that he couldn't see his killers. I couldn't see mine either.*

Well, so much for old Victor. I had the .50-caliber and didn't feel so alone anymore. That baby could cut down a good-size tree. Sure enough, around midnight the little lights showed up. There was no one to tell me what to do or what not to do. I've never fired this type of weapon before and I imagined it made lots of noise. And make a lot of noise it did. I fired it in short bursts, as I was trained to do on a .30-caliber machine gun. I banged away at a great rate. I didn't feel quite so scared.

I felt a hand on my shoulder and damn near jumped out of the foxhole. It was my squad leader. He wanted to know what I was firing at.

"Those lights."

"Where did you get this thing?"

"Right here. I'm sick of getting shot at."

"You may not have hit anything, but you sure scared the hell out of them. We don't fire at night unless fired upon; if we do the enemy will know our position."

"If they knew where we were last night, they sure know where we are tonight."

"Lay low for now." He then disappeared.

I've never heard anything make that much noise, but I sure was getting fond of that weapon. There were no more lights. I was not scared anymore.

---

16 December 1944, 10:00 P.M.

We are now walking down the road, probably getting close to the bridge. Our brilliant leaders could have had the engineers blow the bridge, but there she stands and now we know why.

---

13 November 1944

My mind went back to that German pillbox and our two men who were still there. It must have been located somewhere to the left of this road. This was a bad day for a lot of people.

The lieutenant had told me, "Sergeant, you and half of your men go outside for patrol; your assistant stays here with the remainder of your men."

We joined up in the courtyard. The platoon sergeant told me that we were going after German prisoners. There was one thing above all others that an infantryman did not want to hear, and I had just heard it. Very seldom did we catch an enemy sentry by surprise or capture the enemy without someone getting hurt. All the great heroics in the movies were strictly for the movie fans. If we saw the enemy and they saw us, it was never pretty. More so in the daylight, and it sure was a beautiful day. This trip would be no exception.

We began the patrol formation with two scouts out front. They carried M1 rifles with ammunition bandoliers over their shoulders, and hand grenades. Their job was to lead the patrol and keep it out of trouble. Usually this job fell to first-class privates. These men commanded respect, and they deserved it. They knew where we were going and would find the best way to get us there. They were the eyes and ears and signaled the leader upon contact with the enemy or when reaching the objective. They reminded me of books I had read about Daniel Boone and how he made his way in the wilderness.

Sometimes the scouts even looked like Daniel Boone. They usually drew enemy fire. This was a dangerous job. Scouts were valuable. When they're skillful, they're invaluable. So much depends upon their skill and judgment. We lost many of them.

The platoon guide came next with an M1 rifle, bandoliers, and grenades. Sometimes he followed in the rear. He was the equivalent of an assistant platoon sergeant; they worked closely together. A guide was a staff or technical sergeant who had come up through the ranks. If he had been around for a while, he was a blessing.

Next was the platoon leader, a first or second lieutenant, depending on his longevity. He carried a carbine, a Colt .45, and grenades. The platoon leader was supposed to give the orders and the sergeant saw that they were carried out. The platoon leader and the platoon sergeant were closely allied. The platoon sergeant was really the key, as he usually had all the combat experience and general know-how. He did his best to keep the officer out of trouble, which also kept us out of trouble. We learned to depend upon the platoon sergeant. Infantry platoon sergeants were technical sergeants, highly regarded and worth their weight in gold. He carried an M1 rifle, bandoliers, and grenades. He was our backbone; don't leave home without one.

The reason for this was simple: a platoon sergeant came up through the ranks. By the time he had earned five stripes, he had had combat experience and been around for some time. He had already been a squad leader and understood the duties. He had also been a rifleman and knew the hazards. Just the fact that he was still alive spoke for itself.

On the other hand, infantry replacement platoon leaders were usually fresh off the boat with little or no combat experience. They didn't really know how to stay alive, but they were supposed to lead forty men. When a platoon leader was new, he was a detriment and ripe for the casualty list. If he hung on, he was promoted to company commander. Either way it was a high-turnover job.

As the squad leader, I was next, a buck or staff sergeant, carrying an M1 rifle, bandoliers, grenades, and a knife. At this period during World War II, there was little chance that today's infantry squad leader had come off the boat with the same grade. A squad leader directed and led eleven men. He was combat experienced and had come up through the ranks, by attrition. Today, we had no assistant squad leader. The combat infantry division was built from the base of competent squad leaders.

The radioman, a private, stayed close to the platoon leader, carried a Colt .45, and hoped he wouldn't have to use it.

A first-class private or corporal carried a Browning Automatic Rifle. This is a heavy, cumbersome weapon that makes considerable noise when fired. It poured out .30-caliber bullets similar to a light machine gun. Because of the noise it creates, it often drew enemy fire. For this reason, some soldiers were reluctant to carry the BAR. But the firepower of this weapon was most welcome in a combat squad. When the enemy heard that noise, they knew exactly what it was and, more so, where it was. This in itself was dangerous. The ammunition carrier, a private, handled the bulky ammunition clips for the BAR man. He also carried a Colt .45 or M1 rifle and was ready to take over if the BAR man went down, which they often did.

In the rear followed any number of riflemen the platoon leader designated. These riflemen were privates. They carried M1 rifles, bandoliers, and grenades.

We were a patrol of eleven. We proceeded north on the macadam road toward Clervaux, then turned east toward the border. Did anyone really know what lay ahead? I didn't think so. We were out looking for trouble. Soon we were in a dirt roadbed, about five feet deep, offering good cover. Both scouts were ahead of us somewhere. I couldn't see them. But I wasn't in charge. We had a rifleman out on each flank and we were spreading out and apart. Everything seemed to be going according to the book. So far, so good.

From experience, I knew that when we contacted the enemy, we shot them all and tried to capture the ones who were still alive. That seemed simple enough, if the enemy held still for all of this; if not, it could end up bloody.

We stopped for a break, and the leader studied his map and checked his compass. He pulled the flankers in for a talk. He and the two platoon sergeants looked over the top of the embankment. Nothing. We started up again, the flankers out. No one had told the scouts that we were stopping. They might be way out ahead of us, maybe too far.

The leader sent the guide out to find the scouts. We continued to move. Just then one of the scouts yelled, "Pillbox!" A German machine gun cut loose. It cut down the platoon guide and one scout. The scout cried out that he was hit. Nothing from the sergeant; he's dead. They were both in a minefield. The sign sticking in the ground illustrated the German word Minen *with the mine sign. The flanker on my left screamed; he was hit.*

The rest of us are in the roadbed. My adrenaline jumped and I yelled at the nearest man to come with me, that we would get the wounded flanker. We crawled up and over the embankment. The man had blood all over his left leg and he was crying for his mama. He was hurt bad. The machine gun continued to blast away. Machine guns are a nasty weapon. They can obliterate a group of soldiers in a heartbeat. When you first hear that ghastly noise, you were either hit or about to be hit. The machine gun was a killing machine and it was efficient. Sometimes the Germans used them for mass extermination.

We crawled on all fours and grunted while pulling the deadweight of the soldier across the field and down off the top into the roadbed, out of sight of the German machine gunner. My face was covered with sweat and my hands were bloody. I was breathing hard. We must have been crawling on the ground just below his field of fire.

A GI cut the wounded man's pants. His left leg looked like it was held together by a little flesh and some skin. Someone gave him a shot of morphine and poured sulfa all over his leg. The sickening-sweet smell of his blood mixing with the stench of exposed human flesh brought my stomach up to my mouth. I vomited, spit, and kept going. I am a soldier. It never looks any better; it always looks the same, like something from the butcher shop. I wondered when I was going to look like this, or worse.

The platoon leader yelled to pull out. With that, three of us ran, carrying the wounded man away from that machine gun. I held him by the shoulder and head while another man held him under his hip and right leg; the third man was carrying his left leg. The leg didn't look like it belonged to the body. We got back on the macadam road. We waited: the jeep with the medic arrived and took away the wounded man. We all had the same thought: When I get it, I hope we have a radio and a jeep.

We headed back to the barn. Every one of us knew there were two GIs back there.

Not one of us had fired our weapon. The platoon leader was too busy running away. He was wrong; one of those GIs might have been alive. We arrived back at our home base and dispersed. I went into the kitchen to get some water. I heard this awful yelling. I looked into the front room; our platoon sergeant, Mose, was under the table, yelling and screaming. I asked if I could help him. He yelled he wasn't going out again, ever.

I summoned the platoon leader, who was on the phone to company. After a while three medics put the platoon sergeant in the jeep. He was still raving as they drove off. I never saw him again. The poor guy. He had done his job. Now he was in terrible condition. I would have liked to think that someone took the time to thank him. I'm sure he was on his way home. Home was where he belonged, not in this madhouse.

The following day, the jeep returned. This time, our platoon leader left. He didn't come back either. That left me in charge.

A German pillbox is twenty-five feet wide, forty-five feet deep, twenty feet high, and is made of reinforced concrete from three to eight feet thick. One-half of this structure is underground. Pillboxes are positioned so that the field of fire of one pillbox protects those in proximity. There was only one entrance; a rear door made of heavy steel. These fortifications made up the famous Siegfried Line, guaranteed by Hitler to be impregnable. German soldiers equipped with a 37mm antitank gun, machine guns, rifles, and grenades manned these pillboxes. When pillboxes are defeated, it's not from the front. It's done by blowing the rear metal door with TNT attached to a long pole. We called them pole charges. This was very dangerous work. The TNT was effective; getting there and back was the hard part.

The company commander called me in to company headquarters. He told me I would receive a few replacements, but that we weren't going to be up to full strength. Our manpower chart showed that we should have had a full rifle platoon of three squads and a heavy weapons squad. We had only one squad. He said he was pleased with the way I had turned the ex-cons into soldiers. I didn't explain my method of training. He said he had promoted me to staff sergeant; that would make me platoon sergeant when we were back to full strength.

Also I was scheduled December 18 for a week in Paris. I had top longevity in the company. I spoke to the supply sergeant; he was from my hometown, Greensburg, Pennsylvania. The company commander mentioned that the lieutenant, our platoon leader, had been court-martialed for leaving the scene of the skirmish without all his wounded. I asked about his disposition. He told me the lieutenant would probably work in supply on the beach. Some punishment. I don't even remember his name.

---

16 December 1944, 11:00 P.M.

Well, here it is, the bridge I looked at from the hill over there in the woods. I stood on that hill above the river and watched the krauts build it. The bridge no one wanted to hear about. I feel strange as I walk across; how many German troops walked in the other direction here this morning? What thoughts were in their heads as they walked toward their doom? They were soldiers just like me. Little did we know they were beginning one of the three most pivotal battles of World War II. Only El Alamein and Stalingrad were the equals of this.

Across the river, we are now in Germany. Throughout history, armies have crossed and recrossed this border. Luxembourg is such a small country. It's taking a licking again in this war.

Without communicating, we all know there is no escape for us. We are in the middle of this onslaught. There seems to be no end of German soldiers. This must be an awesome offensive drive against the Allies.

We now stop for a break; my watch shows 2:00 A.M. We say nothing to each other. Each of us has our own thoughts and fears. Prison camp should be better than combat. We should be alive and well when the war is over. From this view, it may be a long time coming. We are informed that we will spend the night in a barn that is a short distance away. The barn is a welcome sight. We are tired and dejected, the losers, and it's been a long day.

I wonder if the Germans will bury Bill, our one casualty. I hope so. I was greatly saddened when I found him dead. He and I had shared a tent together at the Le Mans replacement center.

September 1944, Le Mans, France

He was a nice young man with a wife and new baby. The two of us were thrown together in a tent for two. We were in the area of Le Mans, France. This was a collection point for infantry replacements headed for combat. All these thousands of troops had recently arrived by boat from the States. In September, we had landed at Omaha Beach after crossing the Channel from Plymouth, England. We knew our fate would be dismal. We would be replacing those who didn't make it. All of us knew only a percentage would return in one piece. Riflemen had a high-casualty future.

We learned to drink Calvados, an alcoholic beverage distilled from apples and strained through hemp. It's a poor man's brandy. We traded soap with the farmers for the stuff. After having heard some horror stories about GIs going blind and dying from this drink, I laid off. My partner and I had a disagreement about something, and I told him I was going to knock his block off. He asked me if I was a boxer. I answered in the negative. He told me he had boxed professionally a few times and it would be no contest. He then showed me a few moves. I was convinced and thanked him for not changing my face. We both laughed and then thought about where we were headed. This sobered both of us. By now we knew we were infantry replacements. I wonder if Papillon felt like this when he was sentenced to Devil's Island.

We had been assigned to a rifle company for combat. I didn't see him after that time until the day before the Germans attacked in Luxembourg. He came into my squad as a replacement, just discharged from the hospital. It was pneumonia. I was so glad to see him. I felt I could completely trust him, that he would be good for the squad. This meant much to me.

And now he was dead. This bothers me. It just won't go away. I'm single with no real attachments but my mother and father, and he has a wife and child. Why him and not me? Does any of this make sense? I wonder if we ever will understand any of this.

---

17 December 1944, 2:00 A.M.

I find a place in the hay, lie down, and go to sleep. None of these Germans are going to shoot me, at least not tonight. I'm so tired I just don't care anymore.

---

17 December 1944, 7:30 A.M.

As the day breaks we are in the farmhouse eating cold sausage and dark bread. We drink bitter coffee. At least it's hot. The bread tastes just as dark as it looks. It has an awful sour taste. Some of the GIs stuff their pockets with the bread, but not me. I don't realize what a mistake I am making. I wonder how the Germans can afford the soldiers to guard us, with such a massive offensive going on. I soon get the answer. The GI next to me tells me how lucky we are, being prisoners instead of being dead. A few of his platoon were captured when their position was overrun. On their way to the border, they passed K Company emplacements. They were located just down the road from us. What remained of K Company was laid out along the road. The Germans may have lined them up and shot them. The Germans had little time for prisoners. At this time we had no knowledge of the famous Malmédy Massacre, where the Germans executed a large number of American prisoners and left them in the snow.

The German captain must have told the general about me when we were lined up. This is probably what saved our skin. I hope the captain gets through all of this safely; he will need all his faculties just to survive postwar. What a waste this all is. All these young people crippled, dead, or mentally injured. We are wasting our youth.

Three of us are told to go into the next room. I am taken around the corner and told to sit down in front of a German noncommissioned officer. He is sitting in front of a desk with my wallet in his hand. My mouth drops open when he speaks to me in a Brooklyn accent. He asks for my regiment and company and how many antitank guns I had. I give him my name, rank, and serial number. He tells me I am going to tell him much more than that. I give him my name, rank, and serial number and tell him he will get no more from me. He tells me he is from "Brooklyn, New York, USA." He is of German parents and he came back to Germany in 1940 to fight for the Fatherland. He tells me that the POW train commander had been the largest furrier in Kansas City. He also chose to leave America and fight for the Fatherland.

He opens my wallet and removes an antitank regiment insignia. Again he wants information. I tell him a friend had sent that to me when we were back in the States and I had forgotten it was in my wallet. He then removes a picture of an old girlfriend and waves it in front of my face. He calls two German soldiers into the room. They are carrying submachine guns.

He says, "I can have these two take you outside and blow off your legs. Do you want to go home to your girl with your legs blown off?"

I tell him, "If you blow off my legs, I still can't tell you what you want to know. My legs will be gone and you won't have something I can't give you. I really know nothing about antitank guns." He tells me we will walk to the train depot, where we will board the train for prison camp. We will sit out the war in safety and comfort. Two men to a room, and Post Exchange with beer, cigarettes, and candy. We'll be playing soccer and softball. It'll be much better than combat. Three meals a day.

I would remember that conversation for a long time.

The two German soldiers escort me outside. My heart is in my mouth. I should have never surrendered. They are going to shoot me. They don't, they take me back to the barn. What a relief! Jesus, what a scare. I inform my squad members what to expect at their interrogation. I can't figure out how that interrogator knew I was a sergeant before I told him. He never did return my wallet, the asshole.

After some thirty of us are interrogated, we are told to fall out. The weather has turned cold and the darkening sky is dropping snow flurries on these miserable creatures. We start off, deeper into Germany and farther and farther away from the American lines. The rolling hills are becoming white and the eerie wind sounds like a moan from the less fortunate. The macadam road winds among the fields just like at home in the wintertime.

We are a long way from home. It begins to get bad when our guards start to search some of us. They are stripping us of personal items, watches, fountain pens, and wedding rings—anything gold. We just keep walking with our mouths shut. We remember the Americans from K Company. These soldiers can shoot us. Next the guards take the galoshes from the feet of those who are wearing them. These American soldiers are forced to walk in their stocking feet. These Americans are noncombatants, as combat troops don't wear galoshes. Some have scarves or cloth in which they wrap their feet. Most of us are wearing combat shoes or boots. These they don't bother with. It is cold and now this country macadam road is all ice and snow. This makes the going tougher. The GIs up ahead are bent over, shuffling along like a bunch of old men.

We stop late in the afternoon at a farmhouse. It's good to sit down and rest. No one speaks; we are all too tired. We are given black bread and water and we fill our canteens, not knowing when we will again have the opportunity. We go on. I feel sorry for those walking without shoes. Each time we stop at a farmhouse, we pick up more American soldiers. The group is growing. Maybe the Germans knew what they were talking about when they said thousands had been captured. I am looking at the German soldier walking beside me. I'm thinking what he would say if I told him that I dropped one of his buddies at eight hundred yards.

17 December 1944, 4:00 P.M.

The icy wind is blowing against my face. I shiver; it's getting colder. My Army overcoat is back in the barn. I wonder who will pick it up. Under my helmet I wear a knit woolen cap, GI issue, that keeps my head warm. My regular shirt, pants, scarf, long underwear, socks, and combat jacket are warm. The missing overcoat is the best piece of clothing issued. Often I have walked all day in the rain and stayed dry. It is also excellent for sleeping on the ground or in the snow. The boots I wear are regular-issue shoes that the old shoemaker at Clervaux made into boots in November.

28 November 1944, Luxembourg

Clervaux, about twenty miles from where I was located before the surrender, was a picturesque Luxembourg town with a castle and a monastery. In peacetime, it must have been an excellent tourist town. There were only older people there; the young ones were gone. These people were warm toward us; we Americans are allies. They hate the Germans. Germans have overrun their country for centuries, twice in this war. Hating was not a word I was familiar with. I knew the definition, but I had never hated anyone. Neither had I known anyone who had showed hatred. These people knew hatred, and hate the Germans they did.

Three of us were housed in a small inn for three days' rest from the front line. This was a reward for our being among the very few GIs who remained alive after escaping the Germans in the Huertgen Forest. The rest, the food, the drink, and the warm bed were most appreciated. This was the first bed I had slept in since August, in the States.

I couldn't remember when I last had a bath in a tub. The smell of the soap and the sensation as the hot water engulfed me were wonderful luxuries. I had become an expert at bathing with cold water from my helmet. (Some called it a whore's bath.) The fresh smell of the bed linen and clean blankets was almost like home. Sitting at a table and eating hot food with a fork and knife had been only a memory. I felt that I was back in the human race.

At nine o'clock, the bar closed and the innkeeper bought us a drink, blessed the duke and duchess of Luxembourg, and thanked the three of us for fighting the Boche. It was a blessing to be clean once again. The barber removed my beard—and removed was the word. He first shampooed, then clipped, and then shaved me. I looked in the mirror and saw this pale person who must have been me. God, what an awful sight.

Again the Germans would be occupying this small country. There's no way I can help them. I can't even help myself. The barber, was he still alive? When the war is over, that Brooklyn interrogator ought to be hanged.

The innkeeper had recommended the cobbler on the hill. After a good hike halfway up the mountain, I found him, a friendly, grandfatherly shoemaker. With his shock of white hair, he was right out of a book of childhood fairy tales, and this forest was the proper setting. He said he had made and repaired shoes for all the people of Clervaux since he was a young man. He would make my shoes into boots so GI leggings wouldn't be necessary.

I watched him as he cut and sewed the leather, changing the Army shoe into a boot. He gave me a piece of leather to smell. He told me that the three greatest aromas in the world are from leather, tobacco, and wood. This new boot was a practical arrangement, as I could now tuck my pants into it. The six-inch length gave the appearance of a para-trooper boot. I had no interest in fashion; however, this new boot would be a tremendous advantage in the mud, snow, and water. He accepted my payment, smiled, and wished me a safe journey. I thanked him and started walking down the mountain road. I felt fortunate to have met this man; I had a nice feeling that stayed with me, until I reached the inn. Then it changed.

We had visitors at the inn, three of them. The shoulder patch told me they were Rangers. Rangers were a special outfit that handled planned assignments other than standard combat. They were infantrymen heavily trained in hand-to-hand combat and demolition. They were masters of all weapons who worked behind enemy lines. They were the elite fighters. They were commandos in the British Army.

"I'm Master Sergeant Smith," said one of them. He added, "You are a staff sergeant, squad leader, Second Platoon, I Company?"

I said, "How do you know this?"

*"We have permission to recruit riflemen for the Rangers."**

I called the two GIs just standing there over. "Do you want to join the Rangers?" They both began to ask questions.

The master sergeant said, "You will be quartered at Division Headquarters, three hot meals a day, sleep in beds, and you won't be on the line anymore. No more foxholes."

"How often do we go out on a combat mission?"

---

*After the war, speaking with a historian of the 28th Division, I learned about that particular Ranger outfit. One hundred twenty-five Rangers were picked to take the German artillery observation installation at the top of the mountain near the town of Schmidt. The historian said to me, "Bill, a Ranger lieutenant told me he was one of a dozen men that came back down that mountain. You can be glad you didn't go."

"No more than three times a month." The two GIs told him they were ready to go.

It never occurred to them to ask why recruits were being taken from the front line. Rangers received special training in the States and in England. Not all Ranger trainees made it. Many were disqualified in training. The training was rigorous and tough. Only the very best qualified. The standard training for infantry riflemen was only three months. This was easy compared to the paratroopers. The Ranger training was far more difficult than the paratroopers, and it was obvious to me they needed bodies to replace casualties; anybody who could stand up was a recruit.

I said to Smith, "What weapons do I carry?"

"Submachine guns."

The other two said, "That's better than an M1 rifle; we're signing up."

"You work pretty close, huh?"

"Most of the time." He then said to me, "You can go in grade, it won't take you long to make tech sergeant."

"I'll bet."

"You'll begin as a squad leader."

"No thanks, I'm staying right here. Good-bye." They all left me behind.

---

17 December 1944, 4:15 P.M.

Walking in Germany this time of year is cold, exhausting, lonely, and not friendly. Where are we going? Are we really going to prison camp, or are we going behind the next hill and line up like K Company? What a hell of a mess. I pick up snow and stuff it in my canteen for water. Our guards are not enjoying this trip any more than we are. They should be thankful they are not back there where the shooting is. I have this feeling that I would be better off back there. At least I know how to be a soldier; I don't know how to be a prisoner. This uncertainty doesn't sit right. Is there really a prison camp? It's every man for himself. I drink from my canteen. The water tastes good even if it is cold. It's all I have.

---

6 November 1944, Huertgen Forest

In the Huertgen Forest, we were bunched up on the side of a mountain. The shelling came in at intervals. "Don't the Germans ever run out of those damn 88 shells?" We had no water, no medical supplies, and no food.

Two of us were in a foxhole together. The branches of the enormous pine trees were so thick we seldom saw the sky. The other man had just returned, wounded, from a combat patrol. His left side looked like hamburger meat and the smell was putrid. He was in a morphine sleep. I felt so sorry for him lying in this wet cold hole, with no idea if he would be buried here or not. But as every dogface knows, better him than me.

I climbed out of the foxhole. The company executive officer was explaining our situation to us. The Germans had surrounded us. My first thought was, No shit. I had just watched the third tank being blasted to pieces as it tried to make its way past the other two broken-down tanks. The dirt path they were on was just barely wide enough for one tank. The Germans had easy meat, just like a shooting gallery. What idiot sent all those tankers to their grave?

It was like watching a show on a stage. It was sickening. Couldn't this Army do anything right? The company commander told us we had no medical supplies, food, or water. I decided I was going to find water for my wounded mate and me. As I walked through the woods with the two canteens, a voice asked me where I was going. Over to the side near some bushes was a foxhole with the company commander in it. I pointed toward an open meadow that had a water-filled shell hole.

He said, "If you look closely, you will see a number of dead bodies lying around that shell hole."

I looked; they were all GIs. He was right. "They went out there for water but a German sniper on top of that hill got them. He's still up there."

"Give me your two canteens. I can fill yours and mine together," I replied. "That bastard has to take a piss sometime." I could run the hundred-yard in 10.6 seconds dressed in a tracksuit; maybe my adrenaline would make up the difference.

I dropped my rifle, pack, and helmet. It was probably seventy yards out there and I wasn't dressed in a tracksuit. I took off, ran straight, and flopped down between two dead GIs. Keeping my head down, I stretched my arms, dunked the four canteens in the water, and filled them. No time to screw on the tops. And away I went. The way back seemed an eternity, with that sniper looking at my back. I waited for the sound of the rifle shot. I thought, Maybe he'll miss this time. I zigzagged like a broken field runner on a football field as I flew back into the woods. There was no shot from the sniper. Man, oh man, was I grateful. Maybe he was taking a piss. The company commander shook his head as he took his two canteens and said, "I would not have done that."

I answered, "Next time it's your turn." I was happy to have the water. Next was a drink for the wounded GI. I didn't even know his name, but he wouldn't go thirsty. And he didn't.

7 November 1944, Huertgen Forest

My two eyes see absolutely nothing in this black. I have no brains and I can't think. My instinct is to survive this night, but how? These thoughts tense my body. I am shivering, it's cold, but I don't know if it's cold tonight or if it's just me. I'm an animal in a hole waiting to be swallowed up. How long will this go on? I can't stand this darkness. I'm trying so hard not to make any noise; I don't want to breathe. I have visions of them crawling through the trees right up to the edge of this hole. I am thinking of the men who were blown apart this morning. I can still hear the awful screaming as the bodies are torn and the bellies are split open with the guts pouring out over the ground, spreading agonizing death around me. They are butchering us.

Is it going to happen again?

In the Huertgen Forest, it was daylight of the third day. We were told the Germans had agreed to have Red Cross ambulances available to remove our wounded. Our outfit was completely surrounded by the Germans. The casualties were heavy and getting worse. The steel frag-ments from the exploding 88 guns and mortars are razor sharp; they slice into the human body with tremendous force as easy as the surgeon's scalpel. The results are horrifying. The cries of agony won't stop. This was one hell of a mess. We had no facility to take care of the wounded, no medicine, no doctors, and few medics. Volunteers were needed to take the wounded down the mountain and deliver them to the German ambulances waiting there. Volunteers would carry no weapons, only the wounded.

It was getting dark, so we had to get moving.

The Huertgen Forest is part of a great forest mass twenty miles by ten miles, the Ardennes. It borders Belgium and Germany in the north near Aachen and continues south through Luxembourg and Germany.

The slopes are steep, the valleys and draws deep. The most pronounced gorge is that of the nearby Rur River.

The forest was covered with a heavy growth of fir trees, some seventy-five, some a hundred feet tall, that held up the sky. Upon entering the first time, I looked up and felt I was in a hallowed place. This forest had been the silent graveyard for soldiers for centuries. It is cross-sectioned with well-defined firebreaks. These firebreaks were calibrated on German maps for pinpoint accuracy of their artillery. The German artillery could literally drop a shell into the coat pocket of an American soldier. And they did, often. The American Army fought every inch of this forest from mid-September to mid-December 1944. The 28th Division alone suffered 6,184 casualties. The division had taken a beating, both physical and emotional.

The thick, dark green fir trees were tall and majestic. In this cathedral-like setting, the snow-topped branches shut out the sky like a roof. These densely interwoven trees covered the gloomy dens of Hansel and Gretel. The wet spongy ground softened the noise of intruders. This is the German Eiffel, which has defeated armies from the beginning of history. From mid-September through mid-December, some thirty-four thousand Americans and probably as many Germans were killed, wounded, captured, or evacuated with combat exhaustion, pneumonia, or trench foot. This ground has been fertilized through time with the blood of soldiers.

We cut small pine trees about four inches in diameter to be used as poles. These poles were then slipped through a buttoned-up overcoat that acted as a stretcher. The wounded soldier was placed on the stretcher and carried by two soldiers. If a wounded soldier had a blanket in his pack, it was used to cover him; if not, he had no cover. Blankets were scarce.

By the time we were ready, it was getting colder and dark as the inside of a box. We formed a single file and watched the stretcher bearers in front. In the inky-black dark, it was one foot in front of the other.

It was slow moving. I kept my head down, looking at my feet so I didn't fall. This soldier was hurt bad. The stretcher was heavy. They say dead-weight is heavier. I didn't know if he was still alive.

Every now and then we stopped and rested the stretcher on the ground. We had no idea how far it was to the bottom of this mountain. Some of the wounded groaned with pain; the more fortunate were in a morphine stupor. It was cold but we were sweating. This was hard work. The footing was bad. Some soldiers tripped and fell, dumping the wounded man on the ground. We stopped again and laid the stretcher down. This was tough, but it must be worse for the wounded. They were carrying lead or steel in their bodies, hacked up to one degree or another; some were bleeding and the blood was dripping on the ground from the wounds.

The wounded had that terrible stench of blood. The smell was sickening. I couldn't get it out of my nose and mouth. It was a sweet and sickening smell. It was unmistakable. I tried to spit it out. I didn't ever want to smell it again. The man up ahead cursed, then tripped over a tree root. I cursed when I tripped over the same root. When in the hell do we reach the bottom? How did we get into this mess? I'm not afraid anymore, just pissed off. After this, I don't think I'll ever be afraid, I'll just be pissed off at all this waste. Our commanders who put us into this mess should be here. Maybe things would be different if some of them were lying on these stretchers.

After an eternity, I felt the ground level out. As I looked up, I saw two German soldiers with submachine guns standing on a small wooden bridge. The ambulances with red crosses were parked on the other side of the bridge. The bridge was about twenty feet long, spanning a small stream. We lifted the stretchers and started for the ambulances.

When I bumped into a German, he grunted. I wanted to kick his ass into the stream. I said nothing. We were adversaries, it was dark, but he had the gun. He moved out of the way and we proceeded. Then it occurred to me that we'd been told nothing about how we were to go back up the mountain after depositing the wounded. It was great that the wounded were to be hospitalized as prisoners of war, but what happens to us?

The answer was obvious; we were not the ones with the guns. Our weapons were at the top of the mountain and we were down here in the valley with the enemy. This mess was just about as screwed up as the reason we got here in the first place. How in the hell did we get surrounded? Imbeciles ran this 28th Division. The high-ranking officers should have been down here with us, with no weapons, mingling with the enemy. Who knows, they might have learned something.

We lifted our wounded into the ambulance and slowly stole away. I wanted to be as far from those krauts as I could. One thing I had learned well in the Army was how to keep my mouth shut and have a low profile. I saw it was a little after two in the morning. Tomorrow would be the fourth day in this graveyard. It smelled of death. Now was a good time to get the hell out.

Next to me was a foxhole. There was a GI in it.

"Move over." I rolled in. Man, I was tired, and it was cold. No overcoat again, just when I needed it. No way could I wear that coat while coming down the mountain with the stretcher. My feet were so cold they hurt. No way I could warm my feet, so I stuck them above my head against the top of the foxhole. My feet would be asleep; they won't hurt. This was stupid; I would keep them there for just a little while.

Something nudged me. My feet were not cold; they were asleep. Wiggling my feet, I was wide-awake. The GI next to me said, "We're leaving."

"Which way?" I asked.

As we both came out of the hole he said, "There is a kraut that wants to go to America."

We met up with another GI and, sure enough: "Here is our German soldier."

79

"It's six A.M. It will be first light in about an hour."

In those dense woods, it wouldn't really be light until sometime later. Sure enough, the kraut wanted to be a prisoner of war and be sent to prison camp in America. He was a scruffy-looking soldier. I searched him; he had no weapons and he was ready. We told him to lead us back to the American lines and we would make all his arrangements.

Off we went, one German soldier, two GIs with no weapons, and one GI carrying a German machine gun he picked up, only Christ knew where. We walked along the mountain halfway between the top and the bottom. My reasoning was that German patrols would take the high or the low terrain, seldom in the middle. There was only one priority: we could not afford to run into any Germans. This journey had to be quick and quiet, if we were going to make it. We made our way through the woods behind the German. He seemed to know where he was going. God help him and us if he didn't.

It was getting lighter and we were afraid that there would be a greater chance to be seen by the enemy. The machine-gun carrier was falling behind. I told him to drop the gun; it wouldn't help us if we saw the krauts. He dropped it and caught up.

We stopped, and the German pointed across the valley to the other side. We all lay down and watched a German patrol, going in the opposite direction. They also were walking in the middle of the mountain. So much for our grand strategy. The next time I escape, I'll take the top. We were so happy the Germans chose that mountain, and not this one. Where is this luck coming from?

The German soldiers were carrying their weapons over their shoulders. Soldiers in combat carry their weapons at port in front of them so they can fire them.

Evidently we were still some distance from the front line. We waited until they were gone, then got up and moved. We were afraid to run since it would create so much noise, as we were knee-deep in fallen leaves.

Our German soldier assured us we were going in the right direction. About a mile later, we heard a shout to halt. The voice was American.

We answered, "Don't shoot, we are Americans, we just escaped from the Germans." We saw some GIs with their rifles pointed at us and we threw up our arms. We were fortunate they were combat veterans; new recruits would have shot us. We lowered our arms and they welcomed us as long-lost brothers, which we were.

We pulled it off, thank God. The German soldier was welcomed also; he would be valuable to our intelligence. We thanked him and headed for something to eat. The battalion commander had no idea that our outfit, I Company, 110th Infantry Regiment, was surrounded about one mile from the town of Schmidt. We described what happened, our location and the casualties, then to chow. We were hungry.

After eating some hot food, I moved to my assigned foxhole. These foxholes were excellent, covered with a roof of eight-inch logs, and they were deep. They looked like engineers had built them. Full of food, legs stretched out, I was soon asleep.

A shout awakened me. The GI standing there told me he was the squad leader, 1st Squad, 2nd Platoon, I Company. I was the new assistant squad leader, promoted to sergeant. The next day we would be transferred to the Luxembourg front.

Just then the German 88 shells crashed into us. In that moment the sergeant disappeared. He didn't make a sound. The shells were pouring in; the noise of the explosions was deafening. I hid in my hole with my hands over my head. Will it ever stop? The shells were crashing in the trees and on the ground. After a while it stopped just as abruptly as it had begun. It always does.

The silence was deadening. The sergeant lay on the ground. I crawled out and dragged his broken body inside the foxhole. He was no longer in human form. He was a piece of meat. He was dead. He had just promoted me and I never even got to know him. I would have liked to, if only for a short while. It happened so fast. It wasn't fair. It was like the gods of war were getting even for the ones that got away, but why him? How long was I going to be lucky? It could have been me. If I had been out of the hole, I'd be lying there with him. Maybe I was next.

After the medics tended the wounded, they carried away the dead. The dead were always the last to go, as if they deserved the final dignity.

The mood was somber during this quiet. The platoon sergeant told me I was the new squad leader. I was now a sergeant, thanks.

"Find an assistant squad leader of your own choice."

One of the soldiers who escaped with me was my choice. From what I had seen in combat, it didn't make much difference who was what. No one stayed around very long anyway. Now that I was learning my trade, I wondered how I was going to get hit and when. Somewhere during all of this, I seemed to have lost my fear. I wasn't afraid anymore. It was an odd feeling. I guessed I didn't have time to be afraid anymore. I'm getting a feel for this; I'm a soldier. I may even get to like it.

---

18 December 1944

This is the second day of our walk into Germany. One of my squad members is walking next to me.

"Look at that," he says. Over in the field about three hundred yards from us is a battery of German 88 artillery pieces, the same type that took so many down in the Huertgen Forest.

"They're using them as antiaircraft guns," I reply. The barrels are pointed toward the sky as the gun crews go through their gun drill.

"They're all camouflaged so they can't be seen from the air."

I mutter, "So that's what they look like."

It's a strange feeling, seeing all this and how it works from this end. Those guns are quiet now, but they sure cause hell on the receiving end. I wonder if any of the German gun crew know just how much damage those shells do when they explode. Have they ever seen the mangled bodies, arms and legs blown off, with only stumps showing and the white bare bone sticking out of a headless body? What fiend could devise such horror? I can tell them what it looks like and the screams that accompany the horror.

The man next to me says, "We won't be living with that anymore. Maybe we will get home in one piece, now. These bastards don't give a shit about feeding us. I'll bet the German prisoners at home get fed."

I'm too tired to answer.

My thoughts return to the cold, as these zombielike creatures trudge along the road. They look like one solid mass of human misery. I figure we walked thirty miles yesterday. We have probably walked ten miles so far today. If we really are going by train, where the hell is it? The farther we walk, the less chance we have of being shot. Maybe we'll get to a prison camp.

We stop again for a break and sit down on the ground where there is no snow. We sit on top of our helmets; they make good stools. The krauts hang together away from us as if we have scurvy. We all look filthy and worn; maybe we do look like we have scurvy. I walk over to one of the GIs who has no shoes and give him my scarf to bandage his feet.

He looks up and says, "Thank you, this will help."

I smile. "Glad to be of help." I'm thinking, *If this is the treatment out here, what happens next? We keep on walking, what else?*

It's now dark and it's colder. I wonder how cold the soldiers without shoes are feeling. I'm tired and my butt is dragging. Did Christ feel like this carrying the cross? He must have been awfully tired and lonely. Compared to that, we have it easy. I wish I were back there in combat. At least I knew what I was doing most of the time and I could reach in my pocket for something to eat. I do have a D bar in each of my two pockets. One for tomorrow if we are not fed and one for emergencies. The longer I hold out, the better I should be.

The D bar is a bar of chocolate about 4x1½ inches. This chocolate is loaded with nutrition and enough calories to compensate for a full meal. We all carry them. They are tasty, and many a time it's the only food we have available. I don't have any K rations on me. K rations are carried in combat, allowing the soldier to eat whenever he chooses.

They are boxed in a waterproof 8x3-inch container and carried in our field pack.

The food is cold. It consists of some crackers, a good size piece of cheese, a can of meat, a fig bar, and a packet of lemonade. The brain that designed this mess must have had a warped sense of humor. The crackers are harmless, but the cheese is Cheddar and very binding. The binding causes constipation. Squeezing my bowels in the middle of a field, when the krauts decide to unload a ton of 88 artillery shells into my temporary position is an almost impossible task. This interruption creates the most bizarre movements known to man. No Olympic event compares to the movement that takes place next. Dropping the toilet paper, holding on to my rifle, with my helmet falling off, I jump into or hide behind whatever cover I can find to escape the exploding shells. Of course, I'm trying to keep my pants from falling down as I trip over them. Bare-assed, I lie there hoping I won't be hit.

I wonder if the krauts can actually see me and I'm the target, shiny bare ass and all? I can imagine the German artillery observer calling out the target. "One shiny bare ass at horizontal 1.6, vertical 13.0. Fire for effect."

Do they issue a special medal for hitting a bare American ass? Possibly.

The fig bar is never eaten unless it is to cure the constipation. Eating the fig bar is asking for a case of diarrhea. We only move our bowels when it is absolutely necessary. We even have olive-drab-colored toilet paper, camouflaged. No one ever issued anything to camouflage our shiny white ass, though, while we are in the process.

The most ridiculous thing is the powdered lemonade. This is dissolved in cold water and consumed in below-freezing weather. The lemonade packs are thrown away, unused. There are also a few hard candies included with this meal. What a joy. No one eats the Spam; we always see a trail of unopened crates that tell us the Americans were here. Spam and Kilroy everywhere. That constituted the main rations of the American foot soldier, the K ration. I could eat half a dozen now.

CHAPTER 3

The Boxcars

18 December 1944

We are still walking. It's dark, it's cold, it's wet, and it's miserable. We look like ghosts moving through the fog. We feel like ghosts and we may end up as ghosts. I feel dirty, my feet hurt, and my stomach feels like a balloon. There is no one to complain to. The Great American Soldier's only true right in this Army is to gripe to someone about something, anytime, and all the time. Now this is gone. No one dares open his mouth about anything. These people don't like us.

We are entering a town. Someone says it's Gerolstein. I see streets, some soldiers, very few people, and the usual drab buildings. It's dark and foggy. Everything that makes up this scene looks gloomy and any movement seems to be in slow motion. This seems to be a dream, though it's not. Small shiny glows are moving around in the dark, making the scene seem even more ethereal. One comes up close to me. It is a shiny metal piece that hangs from a German soldier's neck on a chain over his uniform jacket. He seems to be directing our movement. Maybe he's a military policeman and the medallion designates his status.

The cobblestone streets have sidewalks of flat stone; the shop windows look old European. In another time, tourists would find these shops quaint, but now they just look foreign and unfriendly. No cars appear on the streets and very few people are visible. The townsfolk are probably sitting down to dinner. I don't imagine we will be invited; we are the enemy that kills their children, the monsters. We are invading their country, their lives, and disrupting their families.

I must leave these depressing thoughts and concentrate on how I'm going to get through this.

We arrive now at a large railroad station. The guards herd us into a domed building. When I was a boy I first saw one of these in Pittsburgh; it housed the railroad trains. This one smells exactly the same. It's a smell familiar to those who grew up in the coal region of Pennsylvania, a smell of ashes and smoke. But these are German ashes. It smells like a coke oven. The railroad men called it "the barn."

We join the group of GIs sitting on the floor; there are now a few hundred of us. The floor is cold to sit on, but it's better than standing up. I'm ready to drop. We are all so damned hungry we just don't talk about it. I imagine this is what it feels like to be in a penitentiary. I've just made a firm pronouncement to myself. I will never go to jail if I get out of this. Never.

---

19 December 1944

In the morning light I can see that many more GIs have joined us. There may be seven hundred of us, maybe a thousand; it's hard to tell. I have never been in anything like this. We received no training or education on what happens upon capture.

My bones ache, my head aches, and my mouth tastes like something died in it. I take a drink of water from my canteen; the water has a plastic taste, because the canteen is made from plastic. I wish I could wash my face and brush my teeth. Do the Germans realize these conditions are unsanitary? We should be able to complain to someone, but who? The krauts are yelling at us to move: *"Raus, raus!"*

The man next to me says, "Fuck it, I'm not going anywhere, my feet hurt."

I don't bother to answer him.

We are bunched up like a herd of cattle. Down the railroad track about a hundred yards stands our new home, the standard World War I vintage boxcar, the "forty-and-eight." My father, who was awarded the Silver Star and the Purple Heart in World War I, had described the forty-and-eight to me. He and I were both in the same I Company, 110th Regiment, 28th Division. He was in the First Platoon; I was in the Second Platoon, in different wars. He was crippled his entire life. He walked with a decided limp and was unable to play ball with me during my younger days, as other fathers did with their sons. Now here we are fighting the Germans again. Will my son be over here going through this same ordeal? Not if I can help it.

Forty-and-eight means the four-wheel boxcar is designed to house forty men or eight horses. We are now climbing into our new home, sixty men to a boxcar. It is made of wood. There is room to stand up, but not enough to lie down. We sit on the floor. American soldiers must be the most creative, obnoxious, ingenious, conniving, self-serving soldiers in history, but they are tough, loud, and raise hell like no other nationality. The American soldier is also the best fed and best clothed, and when he isn't, he raises hell about that.

December 16, 1944

My thoughts go back to my barn. That was the last American food I had eaten. A large thermos pot held pancakes, bacon, strawberry jam, and a gallon coffeepot. It was delicious; it even smelled good. If only I had eaten more. The horrible thought is, it's still back there and I can still taste it.

We receive two hot meals a day, which come to us from the company headquarters kitchen. After eating from boxes and cans in a combat zone, this food is a blessing. Two soldiers bring it in by jeep. Since this is an inactive front, no one is shooting. The jeep makes the trip in the afternoon. The noncombat troops feel safer in the daylight. As darkness approaches, they become nervous. They never stick around for long conversations. We never kid them about their bravery, or lack of it. A number of the American soldiers are noncombatant because of battle fatigue; they are completely worn out and will not be forced to fight again. Some refer to these soldiers as cowards. I prefer not to think of them at all.

On the morning of December 16, I had spread jam on my pancakes and wrapped them around bacon. I could eat this pancake sandwich as I moved around during the attack.

Right now I can't think of anything more delicious. I wish I had brought some with me. Aren't these krauts ever going to feed us? The doors are closed; I can hear the bolts being locked. We are in here to stay. Never have I been locked into anything. This totally helpless feeling is not good. I'm not going to like this. It's like being punished.

How do we relieve ourselves? How do we obtain drinking water? When do we eat? Who knows? Most of us are too tired to talk. Some are discussing the manner in which they might escape this confinement. This place is filthy, cold, and drafty. I take a swig of water; it tastes worse.

There is a small opening on the side of the boxcar. A GI is taking a leak through the hole: Yankee ingenuity. There is straw on the floor; it helps keep our buns from being so cold. The train jerks then moves. Some give a cheer. Those clowns are cheering, I'm laughing, and we have no idea where we are going. There is a lot of vocal speculation; the general chatter helps distract me from my depression. I shiver as the cold air pours through the crack and I shiver as I contemplate where I am and what I am.

My watch shows 10:20 A.M.; we have been moving since 8:00 A.M. Everyone is positioning and repositioning, trying to fit into the most restful space. Naturally the big guys move the smaller ones to make more room. It's apparent that survival is the priority. We're enlisted men, noncommissioned officers, and privates. The men from my original squad have stayed close to me. This is good. When push comes to shove, there are eleven of us, tight as glue. I feel more like a gang leader than a squad leader. Maybe that chicken-thief major is on this train. It would be hilarious to see his face again. What, no chickens today?

The train is slowing down. It stops. We sit. I am thinking. Survival—that's what this is all about. In combat or in this situation, to survive is the objective. Get through today, so there is a tomorrow. When the man next to me is hit and goes down, the first emotion I have is, *I'm glad it wasn't me.* The second thought is, *We are another man short.* The third thought is sorrow for the lost comrade. Survival is selfish; it's a real hard emotion.

I look at my watch; I must have been asleep for over an hour.

The train hasn't moved and some of our comrades are speculating about the reason for this. One GI says, "These cars aren't marked on top with a white cross, to indicate neutrality for prisoners of war. It's protection against aircraft, so they don't bomb us."

Another says, "We've got to tell the Germans to paint white crosses on top of these cars."

A sergeant sitting across from me says, "You tell them; they're all over there in that ditch, hiding from our planes."

Some of the prisoners begin banging on the side of the box-car and yelling. Shots ring out; one bullet hits the top of our car. The sergeant says, "You got your answer, wise guy, sit down and shut up before they shoot all of us."

It was quiet; we all were thinking.

In most groups of soldiers there are quiet ones, loud ones, weak ones, mouthy ones, strong ones, and tough guys. I don't see any tough guys.

Hostility hangs over this group like a dark cloud. Comrade-ship is isolated. The eleven of us are tight as glue; we seem to be the exception. I continually look around and size up the others; no friendly faces in this group. I don't trust anyone outside our squad.

It must have been an hour before the train moves again. The sergeant says, "When the planes come in to bomb the train, the engine is uncoupled and heads for the nearest tunnel. It hides in the tunnel until the planes are gone. The engine is more valuable than a train of prisoners." He looks older than most of us and speaks with authority, maybe because he has seen more.

Someone else says, "We're sitting ducks."

"Get used to it, it's not going to change."

We continue on at a speed of about forty miles per hour. A few of the prisoners are trying to figure out the easiest method to open the doors. I pull a D bar from my pocket, break it in half, return one half, and begin eating the other. My men are looking at me.

"Go very slow on your D bars; they may have to last us a long time."

"I wonder where we are going," says one.

The other says, "I just hope we get there, wherever it is."

It's cold in this wooden cage. The body heat of sixty men in this cramped area helps, but the cold air pours in through all the cracks. The warmest place to sit is in the middle of all this humanity, and the most comfortable is against one of the two solid walls. As I look at this group of humanity, I wonder if their own mothers would recognize them. The thought brings a smile to my face. I bet mine wouldn't recognize me.

My eyes open and I see the moon through the slats in the boxcar. The night is clear; the moon's reflection on the water is cold and far away. The train makes a new sound as it crosses a steel bridge. This train doesn't have a whistle. If this is the Rhine River, then we are traveling east, deeper into central Germany and farther from home. Those twinkling stars must be shining down on Niagara Falls, New York, where my parents live. They are worried about their only child tonight. If only I could tell them I am all right and not to worry. It's so quiet now; I pick up the rhythm of the wheels as they speak to me with their *clack, clack, clack*. I am sinking into the darkness.

October 1944, Wooded Area, East of Liège, Belgium

We arrived today by truck and pitched the tents we carried on our backs. We must have been getting closer to the Germans because the truck drivers were scared stiff when they dropped us off. One of them told me, "I can't wait to get out of here, there's Germans up here." We still had no rifles or ammunition and all agreed we couldn't go into combat, but would probably be assigned duty that required no weapons.

One bright light said, "We'll probably just scare the Germans to death by looking at them."

The ink-black night accents the sky to the northeast, lit up with yellow and red. An officer said, "The assault on Aachen has begun." We all had one thought: we're glad to be here and not in Aachen. The sky looks like a combination of the Fourth of July and a tremendous fire; it must have been an inferno.

"Maybe this is what hell looks like," I said to my friend.

"If it does, I'm staying away from it."

I remembered something from old history lessons: "Aachen was the birthplace of the emperor Charlemagne and was the capital of the Holy Roman Empire. Thirty-two emperors and kings were crowned there." What a mess it must have been tonight.

---

20 December 1944

The train stops and we all get out. This sorry lump of humanity begins to move, then gradually develops into a group of individuals. As we climb down to the ground, the guards remind us they are watching us. It is getting tougher and tougher climbing in and out of the boxcar. These old civilian guards should be home with their grandchildren, not here, where they might be killed at any moment.

We relieve ourselves, then line up to fill our canteens from a faucet. No one asks if the water is clean or contaminated. No one cares. War is humbling. We have no dignity, look filthy, feel filthy, and we are at the bottom of the pit. If the Germans are trying to break our morale, it won't work. We have no morale. The snow-covered mountains around us remain cold and hostile. It has been four days now, and we have been fed nothing.

The genius standing next to me says, "Sarge, they're not going to shoot us, they don't have to. We're going to starve to death."

"Shut the hell up." There is no use threatening anyone with punishment or promising violence. No one gives a damn. We just have to tough it out, period.

The German soldiers don't look much better than we do. Some of them look disabled and some look older. They may have been injured in combat and are now only fit for this type of duty. Most are privates, plus a few noncommissioned officers. None of them look happy to be here. They seem to be afraid of the American planes. They may be thinking about what would happen if we all jumped them right now. I know we are thinking about it. If we jump them, some of us will be shot. There is no doubt in our minds that we can take them. The problem is that we don't know where we are. We don't know how far it is to the American lines. I know we are east of the Rhine River because I saw it last night as we passed over.

The man next to me says, "We ought to jump them."

"Do you want to be the first?" He doesn't answer.

We are herded back inside. I take a careful look at the train; it's a long one. I don't know where the guards ride; it must be in one of their own boxcars. The civilian guards carry old bolt-action rifles, while the soldiers carry submachine guns. I'm not afraid of the rifles, but the submachine guns are something to take seriously. The threats of these weapons keep us in line.

97

We are back inside. It seems we get out to relieve ourselves only when the train stops because of American planes in the vicinity; in this case, the engine unhooks and heads for the nearest tunnel for protection. The sergeant knows what he is talking about.

THE BOTTLE

I was deep in thought about our bottle of scotch. I wondered where it was now. That bottle traveled with my buddy and me from Baltimore, Maryland, to Tent City in Le Mans, France. It rode on the French ocean liner Île de France, *packed in with ten thousand American troops and debarked with them on the Clyde River at Glasgow, Scotland. Then it traveled by train to Dover, England. After crossing the English Channel by boat, it landed at Omaha Beach, Cherbourg Peninsula. Many truck rides later, the bottle, accompanied by Pete and me, arrived in Belgium. At that point I was tired of carrying our prize. We had originally agreed to sell individual shots on the boat, for a dollar each. We would make thirty-two dollars. In those days a pack of cigarettes cost seven cents, so that would be a handsome sum to spend in Europe. We finally figured we weren't going anywhere to spend our money. Wise men that we were, we decided to keep our bottle and drink it the first day we hit combat. Pete had the bottle. As we left the truck and assembled we heard the voice that disemboweled our well-laid plans. "All men with names beginning with the letters* A *to* M *over here, all others assemble to the right." There went Pete; there went the bottle. After the war, when I was safely tucked away in college, Pete's letter caught up with me. He and his foxhole buddy did drink the whiskey their first day on the line. His sergeant was in a rage when he found the two of them drunk, laughing and giggling in their foxhole. He sent them back to the aid station, where lots of cold water put them right. Shortly after, Pete was wounded by shrapnel and was hospitalized. He was discharged as a supply sergeant, went home to Carmel, California, and married a wealthy woman twice his age. She was an artist. Pete also was an artist, of a different kind. He was the absolute smoothest ladies' man I ever knew. It was always a pleasure watching him work.*

---

24 December 1944

The sour atmosphere of defeat hangs in the air like heavy smoke. The mood in this boxcar is ugly. These men want to get out of here. This is the fifth day on the train.

Most of the prisoners have eaten the food and D bars they had on them and they grumble that the Germans have given them no food since we began this journey. I have one D bar in my pocket. I am determined not to eat it until I have to. When will that be?

The train is stopping; the doors are open and the guards are handing small boxes to us. We are not to leave the car, so this is not a piss break.

Someone yells, "It's food from the Red Cross." Sure enough, it is.

Someone else says, "Just in time for Christmas, it's Christmas Eve." Everyone is yelling, pushing and shoving. Someone hands me a 12x8x4-inch box. I didn't realize it was Christmas Eve.

"One box for six men, Sarge." We are so happy to see anything that is food.

I yell, "You five guys around me." We open the box very

carefully. Inside, there are small cans: vegetables, chicken, sausage; crackers; and a bar of chocolate make up our feast. Among the six of us, we have two spoons. We pass around the spoons and everyone takes a portion. I taste the green beans, the peas and carrots, then some chicken and crackers. I grow tense as I try to swallow the food slowly. I try to make it last as long as possible. God only knows when we will see food again. What a relief to eat again. Our treatment has been less than humane.

The air is solemn with the seriousness of this occasion, as each of the chosen five is mighty careful how he spoons his portion so no one comes up short. "I'm proud of you," I say. "You're real soldiers." I smile to myself as they grunt and continue eating. I'm developing a fondness for these men; they had become good riflemen when we were still back there.

Although we all eat slowly, this small portion of food disappears in short order. This food box was designed for only one person. We all take a swig of water and look at each other with a smile, then we split the chocolate bar into six pieces, and down it goes. Unfortunately, we don't eat enough for a good belch, but we try. What a nice Christmas present this has been; thank you, Swedish Red Cross, and the decent German that arranged this for us.

We all lean back, close our eyes, and think nice thoughts of home on Christmas Eve. The songs of Christmas begin. Everyone is softly singing. Some begin to fall asleep. I gently drop into the blackness.

I'm dreaming. The noise is unlike anything I have heard before; something is rocking me, something is wrong, and I'm in danger.

"Sarge, Sarge," says the voice next to me. "Wake up, for Christ's sake, it's an air raid," he yells.

I holler, "Where are we?"

"We're in the Frankfurt rail yards."

The booming noise is from bombs that the RAF is dropping on us; the British bomb at night, while the Americans bomb by day. The explosions are horrendous. Our only light comes from the explosions. The closer ones rock the boxcar. I can see through the cracks in the side of the boxcar. We all are down as tight as possible against the floor, waiting for the direct hit.

I wait for the explosion. This is like playing Russian roulette. It's like holding my breath underwater. How long will it last? Some of the explosions rain shell fragments against the outside of the car; it sounds like thrown gravel. Every man is holding his breath, which may be his last. Those huge bombs are designed to destroy whatever they come in contact with, including human flesh. No one has been hit so far; there would be screaming and yelling if anyone were hit. I imagine the train engine has long ago gone into hiding, while we sit here like ducks in a shooting gallery. Those bastards!

Our own allies are bombing us. Of course, they are bombing the rail yards, not us. Those bastard Germans could have pulled the train into the tunnel behind the engine so we wouldn't be in the middle of this. We all have experienced shelling from mortars and artillery, but no one has actually been in an air raid. The bombing sounds farther away now; my breathing is slowing down to normal; maybe it's over. I don't see any searchlights or hear any sirens. The bombs must be doing a job on this rail center. The bombing continues, but it is definitely going away from us. It's now quiet again.

The noise is far away now. Some poor souls are taking a beating and somewhere people are hiding in fear exactly as we were doing a few minutes ago. Somewhere buildings are being devastated, people are being crushed and destroyed by this awful destruction. Out there, the bodies of women, children, and elderly men are mutilated and dying. It is as if this part of the world is being destroyed. God has been good to us tonight. I mumble a prayer of thanks. I may be filthy, tired, scared, and hungry, but I am still alive to face another day. The survival continues. I'm thinking, *I want to get home in one piece.*

It is quiet and dark. A voice in this dark says, "I wonder if the guys in the other cars got through this."

"We won't know until it's light and the krauts let us out of here," I answer.

"Maybe they'll be back to bomb us again," reflects the voice.

There is no answer, and there is a reason for this. Many prayers are being said in the darkness. Heaven is hearing from many American prisoners of war sitting in Frankfurt, Germany on Christmas Eve. I wonder what our parents would think if they knew where their children were tonight.

Daylight brings the guards out of hiding. The doors are unlocked and opened. We all slowly pile out onto the ground. Sitting on that floor twenty-four hours a day takes its toll and we all move like old broken-down men; that's what we are becoming. Our boxcar looks undamaged from this side, but we are not permitted to look at the other side. The top is a bit scratched, but there are no holes. The third car from us has damage. Part of the upper section is smashed. There are a few GIs being treated for minor wounds by a German medic. We all relieve ourselves under the watchful eyes of the guards.

I say to the man next to me, "They seem to be afraid."

"They're afraid of the planes, not us; we can't go anywhere. We can't escape, we're in the middle of Germany."

We are permitted to walk around in the small area in front of the boxcar door. This helps the stiffness. I say to my companion, "They're afraid that we'll jump them."

"I'd love to jump the bastards and shove those old rifles up their asses."

"Then what would you do?"

"I don't know, but it would be worth it."

We are outside much longer than usual this morning. It feels good to be in the open and not in that cage. I almost forgot it's Christmas Day. I'll take combat over this any day. At least in combat there's a break once in a while, but this just goes on and on. On Thanksgiving Day, we had turkey, mashed potatoes, gravy, and vegetables, cooked by the company mess sergeant and delivered in thermal pots.

My stomach begins to growl.

I'd better think of something else. These thoughts aren't getting me anything but remorse.

Why the hell couldn't we have blown that bridge over the Our River?

The man next to me says, "They don't have to shoot us; they're going to starve us to death."

"Keep your mouth shut, that kind of talk won't get us anywhere."

———————————

It is now the twenty-ninth of December. We have been caged in this boxcar for ten days and we have eaten once. Six of us shared one Swedish Red Cross box of food. I didn't have any fat on my body when I started this trip; I must look like a fence rail now, a fence rail with a thirteen-day beard. Thirteen days of filth. I'm getting sick of this. I guess this is an example of feeling lower than whale shit.

It is the general opinion of all concerned here that the absence of food causes the stomach to shrink. If the stomach is shrunk, it doesn't require as much food to fill it. Therefore, the theory continues, eventually we will not be hungry for any food. It's a great theory, except the body does require nutrition to survive. By now everyone has recited all the known recipes his mother or wife has ever cooked. Everyone has also described, in detail, just how each recipe has tasted. We are all getting sick of hearing this. We agree to stop this wishful thinking since it only makes matters much worse. When someone begins again to describe food, there are loud shouts: "Shut the hell up."

Now and then a difference of opinion will occur between prisoners and this leads to a scuffle. It's ridiculous, since there is no room for either participant to take a full swing at his adversary. This always results in a larger prisoner informing the participants that he will level both of them if they don't settle down. This charade is comical since no one has the strength for anything physical. We are realizing just how weak we have become. The Germans evidently decided to weaken us through starvation so we would be no problem to them. There will be no escape from this train.

The train stops. A voice says, "The sign reads 'Bad Orb,' whatever that means."

Another voice says, "It's the name of the town, dickhead."

This is the first town where the train has stopped, maybe we have arrived. Anything will be better than starving in this damn boxcar. It's 7:30 in the morning, the twenty-ninth of December. The bolts are released and the doors open. We are piling out like a bunch of cattle. Sure enough, the sign says BAD ORB.

This pretty red-brick railroad station is a surprise; with its bright green-and-black trim, it looks cute enough to be under someone's Christmas tree. Pushcarts are outside standing at attention, ready to handle the luggage of passengers from another day. This picturesque scene has no civilian traffic scurrying to and fro; the only thing that ruins the tranquility is the German soldiers. These people are at war.

CHAPTER 4

Stalag IX B,
Bad Orb

29 December 1944

We are lined up in columns of four; the train guards are gone. The prison guards are easy to spot with their clean, smart-looking uniforms. They are well organized and perform their duties with military precision. I take one last look at those gruesome boxcars. The one in which I spent the past ten days is out of sight.

"One step at a time," I tell my companions. "Keep your eyes open, your mouth closed, and stay away from troublemakers."

German soldiers give the order to march forward and away we go. Privates and noncommissioned officers in their blue or gray uniforms wear an American-style overseas cap; the officers in their gray or green uniforms wear a visor cap. We must look like Willie and Joe from Bill Mauldin's cartoons. I wonder if the Germans have ever read the *Stars and Stripes*? Evidently we are a good distance from a combat area, as there are no steel helmets in sight.

Bits of information come to me through some of my squad members who speak and understand the German language with some level of competence. They attempt to talk with the German guards. I'm going to need all the information I can get if we're going to get through this alive.

"This is Bad Orb, a tourist town, in peacetime known for the healing waters," comments a GI. As we proceed to walk around this little town, I take a position in the middle of the formation away from the guards. I remember only too well how the first guards stole from us; however, I still have my shoes and my watch, and I intend to keep them.

My German-speaking comrades are on the outside of the formation, closer to the guards. The Germans like American cigarettes and the easiest way to strike up a conversation with a German is to offer him one. It's amazing to me how many cigarettes are floating around. I don't smoke, so I have none. We leave the edge of town and proceed up the mountain on a macadam road.

Just about the time I'm thinking, *This reminds me of the countryside at home*, a group of schoolchildren are passing us in the other direction. Seven or eight years old, they have their schoolbooks in knapsacks over their backs. I think to myself, *Why weren't we smart enough to carry our books like that?* They wave to our guards, and they give us a questionable look. We are probably the first Americans they have ever seen. They look healthy, well fed, and intelligent. Evidently they are much too young for the Army. Hopefully, the war will be over before they're old enough to be destroyed or crippled. We continue to walk up the mountain through the snowy pines. It's cold and my stomach aches. I wonder what are we getting into.

As I take a swig from my canteen, I reflect, *I'm sure glad I brought this with me.* This must be the camp. It looks ugly. A barbed-wire gate blocks our path. The outside fence looks to be twelve feet high, with about twenty feet of space to the second fence, which is the same height. The inside fence is completely barbed wire. We stop at a small wooden guardhouse. Our guards speak to the gate guards. Just like the American Army, hurry up and wait. We're at the top of the mountain; it's much colder up here.

"Home sweet home," says John. All my squad members are close by.

The Germans may not be the tough part of this deal; it may be our own GIs. This is going to be a test of survivorship to see who comes out of this alive. Don't trust anyone. These GIs are a cross section of humanity, some are good, some are rotten, and some in between. We stick together and help one another. That way we will have a better chance than most.

The prison guards in the towers wear steel helmets and look all business. We proceed into the camp. The barbed wire and guard towers with machine guns remind us who and where we are. I feel a dark premonition; something bad is going to happen here.

Over to one side I see an American colonel and some other officers speaking to several German officers. Could those American officers be our regimental commanders? We are ordered into a building that's empty and cold. The guard directs us to a pile of blankets. We pass in single file and are given two blankets each, one for over and one for under. These blankets have seen much wear, probably discarded from use, but are better than what we had on the train. I wonder who may have used them before. We look at each other. Where are those who used these blankets before us now?

"Where are the beds?"

"There are no beds. We sleep on the floor."

The bunch of us grab space next to the wall.

"It's safer here, there's no one behind us," I tell them. We remove our helmets, but keep our knit caps on our heads. There is a ruckus going on over on the other side of the room. "Stay here," I say, and I walk over.

Wouldn't you know it, a craps game is in full progress. GIs are swearing, cursing, and throwing money around like crazy: French francs, German marks, English pounds, and, of course, American dollars. There are about thirty GIs. Now they're selling watches and gold rings to cover the bets. Yankee ingenuity is in full swing. It looks like a pawnshop just opening for business. None of us have enough money to gamble.

I walk back to our end of the building. John and the squad members are discussing the latest. It seems one of our group has grandparents who live at the foot of the mountain in Bad Orb. He is telling my squad members that he's had enough of this.

"I'm going home to my grandparents, I'm not staying here any longer." He walks over to the guard and speaks to him in German, and they go out the door together.

We never see him again. Weird.

As it begins to turn dark we are ordered outside and form a single line to be fed.

Most of us use our helmet or canteen cup for the soup and the slice of bread. The soup is water, with dehydrated greens and no meat. It's not soup, but it is warm and the bread is black. We all gulp it down as if it were Mom's home cooking. We haven't eaten since Christmas Eve. Tomorrow is New Year's Eve. We are given a cup of black hot liquid that we pour into our canteen cup. It's wonderful to put something in our stomachs. The liquid tastes odd; it is made from chicory, a substitute for coffee. It is appreciated. We are permitted to fill our canteens with water from a single faucet, then we find the latrine outside our building. We can't see anything else in the dark.

The craps game comes to a halt as the lights are extinguished and we settle down for the night. This is better than starving in that cold boxcar. We can now lie flat with our legs stretched out. It feels wonderful. It's been ten days since I could lie down with my legs straight. We tie our shoes around our neck so they can't be stolen. The helmet becomes a useful companion. We eat from it as from a bowl, we sit on it as a stool, and we turn it upside down and use it for a pillow. In combat, it is our personal protector. Whoever designed it did a really good job. I thank him. It must be cold outside; I snuggle into my blanket as the howling wind sucks me into the darkness.

It is 8:00 A.M. and roll call. The indoctrination is about to begin, and we all move toward the field in the center of the camp. We are in a parade formation, standing in a foot of snow. The military discipline must be the same for both armies: rise and shine.

The camp commandant is introduced to us. He looks beautiful in his gray uniform. I remember the first German officer I ever saw, in a gray uniform.

Early October 1944, Huertgen Forest

I saw my first dead German lying next to a tree. Dressed in an immaculate gray officer's uniform, his stone-cold body looked like a figure in a wax museum. A handsome man with blond hair and a clean shave, about thirty-five years old; he was probably from the upper class or aristocracy. How do they keep so clean? Lying flat on his back, he seemed to be napping. I expected him to open his eyes and sit up, but he didn't.

His cap was lying next to him as if it just fell off. I didn't feel any empathy for him, for he was my enemy. He was just one more we didn't have to kill. His polished boots had a bit of dirt on the sides. There was not a mark on him. He must have been hit from behind, or killed by concussion. I thought to myself, So that's what they look like up close. I wondered if his family knew where he was. Someone has just lost a father or a husband. My grandmother emigrated from Germany. Could we be related? These thoughts stayed with me as I continued walking into the woods following the man in front of me.

BAD ORB

This German officer also looks well fed. He speaks decent English without the use of an interpreter. He's about fifty years old. He must have done something terrible to be assigned here. I would think the Germans need all the good men they can find for combat. He's probably happy to be out of the fighting.

"This is a penal camp for prisoners who are not able to live within the standard rules of a prisoner-of-war camp. All newly arrived American prisoners will be separated into three groups. Officers, noncommissioned officers, and privates will be interned into different camps. No one will remain here."

We will be fed twice a day, morning and evening, be housed in these buildings until departure, and then be transported to the permanent camp as soon as transportation is available.

We are marched back to the building and I have the opportunity to look around. This is a dismal-looking place. The guard towers are evenly spaced so that each covers the field of fire for the other. As I mentioned before, this is exactly the way the German pillboxes were positioned on the Siegfried Line. The Germans are an orderly, disciplined race; still, I don't like them, even though my heritage is 75 percent German.

It's snowing outside. Along with our morning chicory/coffee, GIs bring large wooden tubs into the building. We line up in single file. Then a GI pours this warm brew into my canteen cup. We take our time drinking, for this is all we have. Two guards with the coffee detail carry bolt-action rifles over their shoulders. The guards and the detail leave. No one mentions the GI who left for his grandparents' home and no one cares.

We are permitted to walk outside. We have only our field jackets to protect against the cold. The knit caps are warm and we keep our helmets with us so they won't be stolen. A couple of fistfights broke out last night, but no one paid any attention. We are on top of a mountain for sure. It's covered with snow and pine trees, much like the Huertgen Forest was. I can't get that place out of my mind. We go back inside; it's a little warmer here but there is no stove for heat, just body heat. I think to myself, *It would be colder today in a foxhole waiting for the krauts to come at us and then we would have more casualties.* We pass the day talking and sleeping. The floor is hard and it's getting harder. My rear end must be shrinking. I think about my rear end and the time I slid down the mountain.

Early November 1944, Huertgen Forest

I crawled up, then out of my foxhole, to relieve myself. In this dead quiet, eight inches of snow blanketed the ground and caressed the tree trunks; everything was tucked in, fresh and clean. No ugliness of war here. The late morning held no activity from the Germans. The sun found its way through the trees and was bright against the snow; it made me squint. I headed for the nearest tree. Instinct told me to urinate under a tree rather than out in the open. I felt exposed with my tallywacker hanging out, as if someone might shoot it off. That would be a dirty trick. Was there a special medal for tallywacker shooting? Imagine a training exercise for tallywacker shooting, like scalp hunting back in the days of the Indian wars. The Indians hung the scalps on a pole like a badge of honor. Where would they hang the tallywackers?

Uh-oh, there was something moving over there.

There were no animals in these woods; they've been gone for a long time. It had to be a kraut. It had to be a kraut because my foxhole was in the forward position, which meant there was nothing between the Germans and me.

I grabbed my rifle, which I had leaned against the tree. I released the safety and edged farther around the tree so I could see. I didn't bother to button my fly. The tallywacker was inside my pants, where it wouldn't be shot off.

There he was, behind that tree. He didn't see me. I raised my rifle. His shoulder was in my sight. I fired, but he moved and I missed him. I heard the next shot. It missed me and hit the tree. It came from over there. Now there were two of them and they were taking off in the opposite direction. There was a third one. I'd better be careful; the three of them could give me trouble. They were over the hill, out of sight, where I couldn't see them.

My adrenaline carried me through the woods, over the snow to the top of this hill. The three of them were going down this snowy mountain to beat hell. The trees were too thick with brush for me to fire my rifle. Plowing through the snow down that mountain was going to be cumbersome. There was a faster way.

Without hesitation I flopped on my butt and began to slide down the mountain on the snow. My rifle was at port position and I was sliding on my behind. This was fun, like a sled ride. I knew I was moving faster down this mountain than the krauts, much faster. What would happen if those three Germans decided to stop, turn around, and blow me away? With that thought, I grabbed the first tree going by and swung around to a stop. I gathered myself together. For a moment I forgot this was a war and those were the bad guys who wanted to hurt me. My enthusiasm was greater than my common sense.

There was no sign of the Germans. This was a high mountain. They were far away by now. They had a long slow hike to get to the top, but a fast trip to the bottom. I was glad they didn't take the time to turn around and put me away. This wasn't the first time I had felt gratitude. Of late, something seemed to be watching over me. I wondered how long it would go on.

I started back up the hill. It was slow climbing with all that snow. Those krauts were on a reconnaissance patrol to see where our front line lay. Now they knew. Even more, they knew where I was. I bet those three were happy they got away without any bloodshed. I knew I was. My buddy in the foxhole probably slept through all of this. He needed it.

I buttoned up my fly.

BAD ORB

It's five o'clock in the afternoon and darkness is settling in. We are in formation on our way to the mess hall, in single file, to receive our rations. There must be about five hundred American soldiers here. We have the same food as yesterday, watered greens and a slice of bread. The kitchen doors are open. Inside is a butcher cutting meat and every one of us sees this. He is standing in front of a block table chopping a slab of meat with a cleaver. We receive no meat; someone does, but not us.

A GI yells, "How come no meat for us?"

The guard tells him to be quiet. We proceed through the line and head back to our quarters to eat our dinner.

"That loudmouth in the tanker's jacket is going to get into trouble."

And he does.

The next morning the coffee crew comes in and we start the day with a breakfast of warm chicory. Just as I have my nose in the cup savoring the aroma, a loud, crisp American voice rings out.

"Give me your attention."

We all look up and there he is. Dressed in a black leather coat with a fur collar and a black fur hat is a handsome, clean-shaven dude with a neat mustache. Unbelievable. How can he look so good, here among all these filthy American prisoners? He goes on to say he is Sergeant so-and-so from such-and-such company, whatever division.

"I am your interpreter and go-between with the camp commandant. Any communication from you will pass through me to the Germans. I live in the guard barracks with the Germans. I will meet with you each morning to make announcements and hear anything you wish to pass on to the commandant. Is there any thing you wish to know?"

His last question got our attention. Mass confusion began. Everyone was yelling at once.

"Where is some decent food?"

"Where are beds to sleep in?"

"Where is the PX?"

"Where is the heat for this place?"

"When do we leave this dump?"

"Where the hell are we?"

The guy then explained that these temporary quarters would remain as is until we shipped to a permanent camp. The Germans had little food for themselves or for us. We had not been expected. Nothing would change until we reached our permanent camp. No one believed this guy was an American soldier. This was just a German trick. If he was an American, he must've been in collaboration with the Germans. He looked suspicious with his healthy appearance and great clothes. He seemed to get enough to eat. All of us wrote him off as a phony.

At that moment the door bursts open and three guards come in with submachine guns at ready.

"Outside in formation," our new interpreter barks.

"Now what the hell is up?" says the man next to me. "Where are we going?" We march to a large soccer field.

"Looks like another speech," comes from behind me. I am getting a feeling of apprehension. I feel like I did when the krauts lined us up at the farmhouse. I'm thinking this doesn't smell right. I don't like lining up. We file into formation, stop, and do a right face, facing the Germans.

The machine gun is facing us. One kraut is behind it; the other is holding the ammunition belt. I say to the man next to me, "They want something, or they would have already shot us."

Our new interpreter isn't with us; he's standing there with the krauts, that asshole.

The German officer says, "Count off by twos."

We comply. "One, two, one, two," throughout the entire formation. I position myself in the second row, I am a one.

The next command comes: "All ones take five paces forward."

The ones move five paces forward. The front row I'm in is fifteen feet closer to the machine gun. This is beginning to look serious. The ones are now in a straight line, about fifteen feet in front of the remaining formation. We remain at attention. I look down the barrel of the machine gun, about fifty feet in front of us. The machine gunner is looking straight into the center of our line. I am standing in the center. He can take us down with his eyes closed.

The officer speaks again. "Last night an American prisoner of war broke into the kitchen and killed a German working there. This German soldier was killed with a meat cleaver. An American prisoner of war has committed murder. This is not an act of war. There are those of you who are aware of this incident. You will step forward and identify this murderer. You have three minutes to step forward with the identification. If no one steps forward, the machine gun will fire upon the first row of prisoners. If there is then no response, the machine gun will fire on the remainder. It is your decision."

There isn't a sound. I look up at the darkening sky. The sun disappears, as if to hide from the hideous act that is about to take place. The cold wind is blowing, like an omen. The menacing silence just hangs there. Time has stopped. Hundreds of men are about to die here. I am thinking, *We are alone with no one to help us. Other men, in history have been in this position, what did they think of during their last minutes? So this is how it feels to be executed. We are absolutely helpless. Being killed in battle is one thing, but this is not necessary. Bad guys are executed; I've been good all my life. This isn't right. My life is in the hands of this German. I'd like to see him standing here in my place. This kraut is trying to extort information from us, but what if no one has any? I don't. I didn't even know the German was murdered, let alone who did it. People die all the time, in war or in peacetime, but not like this. Son of a bitch, this shouldn't happen.*

Two guards suddenly come running onto the field waving some cloth, accompanied by two bloodhounds. The bloodhounds run over to an American prisoner barking and jumping up and down. The guards grab the prisoner and take him up front to the officer. They take him away out of sight. We are all spellbound. This is unbelievable. We all were preparing to die, each of us in his own way and to his own God. And now it's over; we would live. It all has happened so quickly, it is difficult to believe it ever happened. I am stunned. The emotion is indescribable.

"Dismiss."

I am emotionally drained as I stand there and watch the guards pick up the machine gun and move on. The German soldiers turn and depart. We break formation and slowly head toward our building. No man utters a word. Each is deep in his own thoughts. No one hears the wind whispering through the pine trees that it's over. No one minds walking in the heavy, knee-deep snow, and with our heads down, no one notices that the sky is blue and the sun is shining again. The dark clouds are gone.

My German-speaking comrade fills me in. For a few cigarettes, one of the guards briefed him. "That jerk broke into the kitchen, evidently having seen the same meat being butchered that we saw. He's the same loudmouth that was yapping about the meat.

"He and the guard went at it and the guard lost. The meat cleaver was the weapon."

"I feel no sympathy for him, only disgust," I said.

All of us were almost executed because of him. While we all were on the parade ground, the guards with the bloodhounds searched our buildings. They found the bloody clothes. The remainder of the story takes place in front of all of us. We are told that the guilty man was immediately shot. We know now just how cheap our lives are. How close we all came to leaving this world. The despairing thought is that our lives are nothing. We are completely dependent upon our captors. What happened today can happen again.

We have been here six days. The officers have been shipped out to officer land, or wherever they are to spend the remainder of the war. This morning is the first time our interpreter hasn't shown up with his clean-shaven face and fancy duds. No one pays any attention. The craps game has been reduced to about five players. A poker game is going on all day. The poker players have a better handle on the various currencies than do the crapshooters. No one trusts anyone. Last night a prisoner was raising hell because someone stole the bread he was hoarding. This in itself is comical, as we have so little to eat. How in the world could someone not eat what little there was?

This morning the guard tells us that volunteers are needed to chop wood. It seems there is no coal and the krauts use only wood for fuel. For working all day, the volunteers will receive a triple ration of the stew that the guards eat. I sign up, as do all my squad members. At least it will break the monotony, and we can all use any food we can get our hands on. We are to leave before daybreak; just a walk in the country.

We are awakened in the dark. It's cold and the wind has picked up. We stop at the kitchen and receive coffee and a slice of bread. This is better already. There are two dozen of us. We plod through the darkness one behind the other. It must have snowed all night; it's above our knees. After pushing through the woods for an hour, we reach our destination. The trees are predominately pines, with a few hardwoods. Our guards hand us our tools. We have long- and short-handled axes, saws, and sledgehammers. The guards explain to our German-speaking comrade what to do and our comrade explains it to us.

We break up into pairs. Two men cut down a tree with the ax, cut away all the branches, saw the tree trunk into specified lengths, and then split the logs. The lengths are then stacked into a cord of wood. This is all new to me, but I'll remember to my dying day the dimensions of a cord of wood: eight feet long, four feet wide, and four feet high.

The gray light gives way to daylight as we begin. It's cold, so we all keep moving. As soon as a prisoner slows down, a guard is there, giving him some incentive with the butt of the rifle. Although I began by wearing my helmet, I quickly remove it. It is too heavy on my head. We all wear our GI gloves. I begin to feel my hands blistering. We take a break occasionally. I begin to get a rhythm with the ax. Sawing is easier. Splitting the logs with the sledgehammer and wedge is mighty hard work. In spite of the cold, we are all sweating. We are earning our bread.

At noon, we break for something to eat. The stew is good, with some kind of meat, vegetables, and potatoes. We are issued a full canteen cup. This is the only decent food I've eaten since our capture. No wonder the guards look so healthy. We are all glad we came.

After our lunch break, it's back to work. The cords of wood begin to appear. The Germans must use a tremendous amount of wood. This forest is very thick with trees. In the afternoon we all begin to slow down our pace and take breaks more often. The guards are well aware of our usual diet. They are also aware that we've been weakened by this diet, and therefore less prone to run away.

It begins to grow dark. We stack our tools and proceed through the woods to the camp. There are no incidents. We all remember the one who was executed yesterday.

The trip back is longer and we're tired plodding through this thigh-deep snow. The krauts got their money's worth today. We stop at the kitchen and receive another canteen cup of the same stew, which we eat on the way back to our building.

This makes the trip worthwhile. This food makes a tremendous difference.

The next morning when we are lined up for the coffee, something is different. The interpreter doesn't show. This is the second morning he hasn't appeared. The guard is talking with my German-speaking comrades. My comrade turns to me.

"Our interpreter was shot two days ago. The Germans found dynamite hidden under his mattress," he says. "It seems the Germans were making a surprise inspection of the guard barracks. They inspected his room as part of the normal routine, and there it was. They never did understand what he was going to do with it."

This makes a total of three Americans who are no longer with us. Each execution was the result of an entirely different incident. Who could have foretold these bizarre happenings? What's next?

I feel guilty about the interpreter. He really was an American. I wonder what he was doing with the dynamite. Maybe he could have used a friend. I wonder where the American with the German grandparents is now.

This is the seventh day.

The guard comes into our building. "All noncommissioned officers report outside immediately."

A bunch of us group together outside. We are to march out

the gate and down the mountain to the train station. We will leave at once. My squad members pour out of the building.

"You can't leave us."

"I don't have a choice," I answer. We stand there looking at each other. It's sad. "You all have been fine soldiers. I'm proud that you have served with me," I add. "We can get through this and all go home in one piece."

It's an awkward moment, a precious moment. I have a lump in my throat. I'm not prepared for this. I feel bad. I feel I should stay and protect them. No one wants to shake hands. I hold out my arms and hug each one of them. We have tears in our eyes, and I am gone. We have been through a lot together and we are still alive. I never saw them again.

USA

Besetztes Gebiet
Territoire occupé

Südfrankreich
France méridionale

Nichtzutreffendes streichen
Biffer les mentions inutiles

Kriegsgefangenenpost
Correspondance des prisonniers de guerre

Postkarte Carte postale

An
A

recd March 7-45

MRS. EE MELLER - 2227

Gebührenfrei! Franc de port!

Absender:
Expéditeur:

Vor- und Zuname:
Nom et prénom

SGT. WILLIAM F. MELLER
25727

Gefangenennummer:
No du prisonnier

Lager-Bezeichnung:
Nom du camp

10900 U.S. C.C.R.

siehe Rückseite
voir au dos

Deutschland (Allemagne)

2227

Empfangsort: INDEPENDENCE
Lieu de destination

Straße: NIAGARA FALLS
Rue

Land: NEW YORK

Landesteil (Provinz usw.)
Département

Kriegsgefangenenlager M.-Stammlager IX B.
Camp des prisonniers BAD ORB
Datum: JAN 9, 1945
Data

Dear Family: This is the type of card of which I can write to you 4 per month. I am fine + just waiting to get home. Keep all mail + pkges coming as possible. Add graham crackers + baked beans to my list. Don't worry about anything. I can send only 2 letters plus cards, be sure to keep writing. All my love. J. P.S. Hello to Frank.

The Swedish Red Cross provided postcards for the POWs
to mail home to the United States. They were thankful to the Swedes
for their only communication to the outside world. This card arrived
to Meller's mother after he came home from Europe in May 1945.

COURTESY OF THE AUTHOR

Stalag IX, Ziegenhain

Above me, low, black, menacing storm clouds pour out of the slate sky as if to cloak this dark, vile picture from view. I shiver at the ugliness that permeates this bleak, repulsive structure: a large kennel with guns and barbed wire, a place to avoid, and I'm on my way in. It's a prisoner-of-war camp.

Entering the main gate, we see the guards are both German soldiers and civilians. While the soldiers carry pistols on the belts of their green uniforms, the civilians carry bolt-action rifles that look like World War I vintage.

"I wonder if those old rifles actually work," says the man behind me.

"You don't want to find out," a voice mutters.

"It's nice they don't carry submachine guns," I add.

Some of the soldiers are disabled and a few are old enough to be World War I veterans. Maybe they knew my father. Farther to the rear are civilian guards, *Grosspapas,* as in Bad Orb. We stop while our guards turn us over to the prison guards, then pass through the gate and walk twenty feet on to the next gate. The two-hour truck ride from Bad Orb is probably our last one.

This gate is a large wire fence with a wood frame and stands about fifteen feet high with a guardhouse on the outside. This gate comes together like two doors. The perimeter is a double barbed-wire fence about twelve feet high that goes on and on until it's out of sight.

I'm dragging and getting sick and tired of this mess. I want to do something. The cold and overcast January day is depressing; even the chilly wind smells musty. These buildings look as if they have been here a long time, probably military barracks. Farmland, for raising crops, surrounds the entire area. The nearest woods is about a half mile away. I can see the edge of the town of Ziegenhain from here, all open land; it must be about a mile away. I wonder if the people in those houses are better off than I am. Do they understand what the future will bring for them?

The guard towers reach up above the fence and the guards look like black vultures peering down at us as if we were new targets. Each tower houses the standard guard and machine gun. Different from Bad Orb, the buildings are constructed alike and positioned in strict geometric order. If they had ever been painted, it was a long time ago. They are spaced evenly and are in groups of two, contained by a fence, which separates them from the next two. These look like the barracks in an American infantry basic training camp, except for the barbed-wire fence between the barracks and the locked gates. There must be other prisoners; I wonder about their nationality. I'll bet some Americans are here.

I am alone now and my former squad members are off to their camp, somewhere. Alone, I will have to learn German or depend upon others. This is going to be tough until I locate someone I can trust. We all are noncommissioned officers from all parts of the service. There are riflemen, tankers, artillerymen, antitank men, intelligence men, cooks, clerks, truck drivers, engineers, and men from supply, reconnaissance, and communications. This is a cross section of the American Army; all are trying to stay alive until the war is over. Some are combat experienced and some have never fired a weapon. What we have in common is that we're all tired, dirty, unfed, and want to go home.

We walk down the main street with compounds of barracks on both sides. Everything is dirt, no pavements. The compounds come right to the street. The French soldiers are talking to us through their fence that faces the street. The French language is so pretty to hear. They want American cigarettes. I wonder, *They're so well dressed. How do they keep so clean?* A group goes by us carrying picks and shovels. They look filthy and sound Russian.

I say to the German guard, *"Russki?"*

"Ja."

We never did see Russians or any other nationality at Bad Orb; where did they keep them? We heard the Russians were locked up tight.

Our formation stops. A group of us turn left through a compound gate and into a one-story barracks and go inside. We walk along the wall with windows. The opposite side has three-tiered bunks from wall to wall. I grab a top bunk. I figure the higher the warmer. It's cold, no heat in this place. The wooden bunk has a few slats supporting a six-foot-long bag, my mattress, which is filled with excelsior, the material used in packing crates. Two worn blankets lie on the bunk. I wonder who slept here before me and where he is now.

"This is better than sleeping on the floor," I say to the man next to me.

"Better than the train," he answers.

"The French have cigarettes," someone yells, and everyone

scatters outside to the fence. I don't smoke, so I continue my walk through the building. The windows have barbed wire. Some have glass and some are covered with wood. We have one small pot-bellied iron stove in the middle of the barracks and alongside it is a small coal bucket with nothing in it. Nothing is in the stove either. It's cold, it's smelly, and it's gloomy. My stomach rumbles.

The latrine is next, with some metal washbasin-like sinks and one faucet in the center. The faucet works but the water is cold, like everything else. Staring up at me is the concrete floor that completes this dingy, foul-smelling room. I can see the outhouses through the window; this is just dandy. I'd like to kick hell out of that Brooklyn-speaking German interrogator. What did he tell me? Two men to a room, and three meals a day. Through the window I see my next-door neighbor. Outside our fence is a narrow street, and on the other side of the street is a long building similar to this one except it has a covered porch running alongside it. *"Bonjour"* comes out of nowhere. I look and there he is: a black face; he is dressed in an undershirt and pants from some kind of a uniform.

He is standing on the porch smiling at me. I think to myself, *Maybe this is Gunga Din?*

What a sight. No one has smiled at me for months and I had almost forgotten the feeling of having someone smile at me. A big smile comes over my face and I say, *"Parlez-vous français?"* He rattles back some French sentences. A sheepish smile comes on my face and I say, "Do you speak English?"

"Oh yes, I have learned to speak English here in prison camp, how do I sound?"

"You sound just fine. How long have you been here?"

He looks up and down the porch, then replies, "Since 1939, when I was captured in North Africa."

132

"You've been here five years?"

"Yes," he replies, "I was seventeen years old." He adds, "My home is in Bloemfontein, South Africa." He is Corporal Simon Moholo, soldier and rifleman from the French African Army.

I finger the D bar I have in the pocket of my field jacket. I think, *This is my last D bar. If I eat this, I'll be hungry for more chocolate later, but there* is *no more for later. Why not give it to him?*

"I'm going to throw something over to you; you'll like it. Can you catch it?"

"I am a very good catcher." I sail it through the barbed-wired open window. The distance is about forty feet and damned if he doesn't catch it. He laughs and says, "What is it?"

"Open it and take a bite," I holler.

He does, and says, "It's chocolate." I explain exactly what it is. He says, "I haven't had chocolate for many years. Thank you."

We are both standing there smiling at each other. It's a wonderful feeling.

"You are American?" he asks. I nod my head. "That is good, that means we won't be in here much longer. Your Army scares the Germans." I tell him I'm glad to hear this. He adds, "The civilian guards are mean, but the soldier guards are not; they just want the war to end. The civilians hate the Americans for the bombing."

He goes on to tell me that he'll smuggle some food to me if I can be on the detail to return the food tubs. Each afternoon, the prisoners from each barracks come to the kitchen and pick up the tubs of soup. After the soup is distributed in the barracks, the prisoners return the empty tubs. He will pass by me on the porch and give me a German mess kit with the same stew that the guards eat. The next day I can return the empty mess kit in the same manner.

"I work in the kitchen right here; you are lucky you are next door." I thank him heartily. He adds, "Keep the mess kit out of sight under your jacket; you may have a mean guard with you." As I walk back into the barracks, I finger the crucifix hanging around my neck.

———————————

Late September, Belgium

No more truck rides, we were walking, one column on each side of this dirt road, headed for the front lines. The road was rather flat and the walking was easy. We were infantrymen trained to walk; a truck ride was a seldom-enjoyed vacation. I felt very heavily weighted as I walked toward my doom; what lay ahead was questionable. We were in the country with fields, farms, and wooded areas; it looked so nice and clean. It was autumn; the weather was mild and the leaves were turning all sorts of pretty colors, just like home. There was no war here.

Would I ever see home again? Would I be buried here? This would have been a nice walk to take with a girlfriend before a picnic, but this was no picnic and I hadn't seen any girls. Although we had seen no combat, we were dressed for it, wearing a full field pack, rifle, ammunition bandoliers, grenades, and steel helmet. We all were becoming tense, thinking about what was around the next corner. GIs were only quiet when they were scared or hurt; no one was hurt and it was quiet.

As I turned toward the bend in the road, I saw a church off to the left in a wooded area. Without any thought I turned in that direction, away from the column, and went off on my own. My steps led me to the front of the church. Standing there on the steps of the church, as if he were waiting for me, was a priest.

"Bonjour," he greeted me.

"Bonjour," I answered. "Parlez-vous anglais?"

"Certainly, can I give you a blessing?"

"Would you please?"

He then blessed me in French and handed me a silver crucifix. I fastened it next to the Saint Christopher medal on the chain around my neck, then vowed never to remove this crucifix from the silver chain and that I would take it to my grave, wherever that might be.

I thanked the priest and hurried to catch up with the column, wishing I could repay this man for the wonderful feeling he had given me. This act of kindness stayed with me, and as I picked up my feet I felt better about myself. The heavy apprehension was fading; I was stronger for what lay ahead.

Ziegenhain

The prisoners are coming back into the barracks; they are loud and noisy. I wave good-bye to my new friend. What a stroke of luck. I jump on my bunk to make it clear to any intruders that this is mine. I feel better for the first time since my capture. I have an ace in the hole, a good omen.

Three soldiers in adjacent bunks begin talking to me. We all identify each other. Most are from the 28th Division. Some are from the ill-fated 106th Division. The 106th Division came off the boat as a complete combat unit, with no experience whatsoever. In combat, they were a complete, disorganized failure. They went down fast and hard. So much for inexperience. One of the three, J. P. Russell, was a pecan farmer from McDonough, Georgia;

another, from New Hampshire, sold maple syrup from his father's maple-tree farm. Each of us is a noncommissioned officer from a rifle company. We have much in common and continue to talk shop and relate combat experiences. These two had been in the Huertgen Forest, but from another company.

"We are about three hundred miles from the Swiss border," says Georgia.

"I don't know how we could get that far even if we could escape from here," adds New Hampshire.

"I believe it's impossible to escape without knowing the German language," I offer.

"What we need," says a tech sergeant, "is information; we can't do anything until we know some things." We agree to sit still and learn more about our captors and our own troops. I lie back in my bunk and remember how it all began.

---

13 October 1944, Malmédy, Belgium

The truck stopped and we all piled out. Someone says, "We're still in Belgium, near Malmédy."

This was a beautiful farm; the large house and even larger barns were constructed of fieldstone. A pretty view swept across the pastureland and wooded areas. Some large Belgium mares were being led into the barn; the clucking chickens who populated the barnyard seemed to be advising us that they were here first. Just as I was thinking that I would have enjoyed living here myself, the noise of the sergeant's bark broke the tranquillity.

"You are being assigned to a unit, here are your weapons," he said.

I took the M1 rifle, ammunition, and grenades; I had forgotten how heavy they were. "You are assigned to Company I, Second Platoon, a Hundred and Tenth Regiment, Twenty-eighth Division."

It hit me: this was the same outfit my father was in during World War I in 1918. What a coincidence this was. He was awarded the Silver Star and the Purple Heart. I would bet he would be surprised to learn this. We were told the 110th was now in reserve and we would remain here until we relieved one of the other two regiments. We all looked at one another and smiled. So far, so good.

Something was going on over by the other barn; it was Company I. The company commander was saying something to the men. He was handing out medals and citations. "Private so-and-so receives the Bronze Star, Sergeant such-and-such receives the Silver Star with Cluster." This meant he was receiving it for the second time; Sergeant such-and-such and Private so-and-so received the Purple Heart. This continued for a while, then the captain made a statement.

"This outfit has run over its allotment of citations for valor. In place of the medals we don't have, we are issuing the new Combat Infantry Badge." He held up one of the badges, then proceeded to hand them out to the proper recipients.

While this was going on, the veteran soldiers of Company I looked as if they couldn't care less. The ones who had just received the commendations looked embarrassed. They stuck the awards into their pockets and shuffled away from it all. They looked like old men.

I asked one of the recipients, "Why aren't you happy about your medal?"

He answered, "The ones that should have gotten them are still laying back there by those pillboxes." He turned and walked away. This was why we all arrived today, fat, dumb, and happy, to replace the casualties. Each of us was sobered by the thought; there were no heroes here.

Ziegenhain, Germany

I meet more members of the 28th who have bunks next to mine. The third tier is soon hopping with conversation. We are soon giving our names and trading experiences with one another. The big question is exactly what our location is in proximity to the American lines. The next question is when will we be found so we can go home. We all look up at the commotion near the front door. An American tech sergeant is asking for our attention. He gets it.

"I am Sergeant _____. I am the American interpreter and liaison between the camp commandant and the American prisoners." He continues, "I speak German and four other languages. Before my capture, I was a tech sergeant/interpreter, in intelligence. I will present any communication between you and the Germans. There will be two meals a day, coffee in the morning and bread with soup at night, same as Bad Orb. A detail will pick up and return the wooden tubs to the kitchen. Elect a barracks leader, and then pull volunteers for duty. One loaf of bread per six men is the ration. Form your group of six and have one man cut the loaf into six slices.

"You can use your canteen cup or helmet for the soup and coffee. If you are found outside your building at night, you will be shot. You will be issued soap for washing and shaving. This plus razor blades and towels have been issued by the Swedish Red Cross. They will also issue Red Cross food boxes similar to what we received on the train. When this will be I don't know. For the present, we will have no outside activity. The Germans are afraid we will escape. The other nationalities here perform work detail, but we will not. There are French, Russians, and Africans interned here. Some have been here since 1939. In late afternoon, we will hear the German news broadcast to the German people. If you attempt to escape and are caught, it means thirty days in solitary. When I have any news or communication for us from the Germans, I will return."

And with that, he was gone.

It's chow time. "We need six volunteers to get the chow," yells the new barracks leader.

Six men go out the door accompanied by a guard as I watch from the latrine window. Sure enough, they walk to the end of the porch and enter the kitchen at the rear of the building. They appear again carrying three large wooden tubs. The tubs are carried with a pole that runs through the two handles, two men to a tub. In the barracks we line up and pass by the tubs in single file and a man with a dipper pours the liquid into my canteen cup. The cup is three-quarters full of soup and I carry this back to my bunk.

"This looks like water with vegetable tops, but no meat," I point out.

"Those are dehydrated greens boiled in water with meat," my companion observes. "Looks like they skimmed ours from the top, the heavy stuff is on the bottom of the kettle," he adds.

We all drink slowly and we are deep in the disappointment of our first meal here. It will hardly keep us alive.

"Maybe they don't want us to live," said the corporal. No one answers him.

The bread arrives and the loaves are spread out on the large table.

"Here is the bread knife," says the barracks leader. "Use it and pass it on." We six step forward. "Six slices, evenly cut, the cutter gets the last piece," he adds.

Each slice is about an inch and a half thick. The five of us watch closely as the slices are being cut. No one wants less than his share. The way we're concentrating can be compared to watching a diamond cutter split a fifty-carat diamond. The cutter gets the last slice; if he makes a mistake, he's out of luck. No one wants to be the cutter.

"It's the same brown bread we had at Bad Orb and on the march. It tastes much better now," I say. We all finish our meal and sit on our bunks. The conversations are about our favorite subject, food, and we are all getting tired of hearing descriptions of Mom's cooking. Most are talking about opening a bakery, a butcher shop, or a restaurant after the war. One thought is in everyone's mind. We will never allow ourselves to be hungry again. We need to get out of here.

Light comes from a few bulbs hanging from the ceiling; it's growing dark outside. We're all lost in our own thoughts and mine are on that tub detail.

"We need six volunteers to return the tubs," barks the barracks leader. He sure is into his new job.

I hop off my bunk. "I'll go."

It's more difficult to round up volunteers to return the tubs. After some complaints and general haggling, six of us head out the door with the tubs. As we walk along the porch toward the kitchen, I bang my end of the tub on the wall to attract the attention of Simon, then yell in a loud voice, "It sure is cold out tonight, too damn cold."

Just then Simon pops out the kitchen door and heads in our direction. He hears me. As he passes me he hands me a German mess kit. It is heavy as I stick it inside my field jacket, then dump the tub. No one sees the transaction, not even the guard. Slick!

I am back in the barracks and onto my bunk. "I've got something for you. Grab your spoon and canteen cup," I mumble to the others.

Instead of the watery mess we had for dinner, this is a stew with small chunks of lamb. We sit there and stuff ourselves.

"My God, where did you get it?" asked the corporal.

"I have a friend next door." I stop all of his questions and explain how it all came about.

"This is unbelievable," says Pete, the maple syrup man. "You are unbelievable."

"Well," I said, "Simon is unbelievable."

I wash the mess kit in cold water the best I can and tuck it in the blankets on my bunk. "We must be very careful and keep this to ourselves," I say. "We can't tell anyone about this," I continue. "Others will find out our secret soon enough. There'll be hell to pay when others find we have a source of food to stay alive and they don't."

It's cold and it's 6:00 A.M. when the lights go on.

"*Raus, Raus.*" It's the guard. He is the civilian with the nasty attitude.

I wake up and slowly roll over. I'm dizzy in the head. I sit up on my bunk with my feet hanging over the side. The others are on the floor. The guard screams something at me and points his rifle. I jump down and he swings the rifle butt at me. I turn to avoid the blow. The rifle butt catches me in the small of the back and knocks me to the floor. I come off the floor headed for the guard when Pete yells, "Hey, you don't want to do that."

He's right. I back off in anger. The guard says something I don't understand then walks away. I make up my mind I'm going to get that bastard, one way or another. This thought is in my mind when we next meet.

After the coffee detail is finished, we are told today is payday. This is news to us. The interpreter arrives, with two guards and a table and satchel. Sure enough, we all line up in single file and move to the pay table. Prisoners of war are paid a daily amount of money for each day in captivity. I receive the few German marks. Before I can put it in my pocket, the guard at the next station holds out his hand and I give it back. So much for payday. We go through this exercise each month. It's a farce. We soon learn the Germans keep the money just as they keep everything else.

Next we are given a few razor blades and some shaving soap. The soap is good in the cold water, but the razor blades are dull. I see a prisoner rubbing a razor blade on the windowpane. "This is the way to sharpen the blade."

He's right; rubbing the blade against the glass does sharpen it. Then with the soap, the blade, and the razor that I borrow I have a clean shave. Using the small towel and the soap, I take a bath in the sink. It's freezing cold, but it works and I feel much cleaner.

The icy wind comes pouring in the open windows, lowering the temperature below freezing. Back in the barracks the potbellied stove is generating a little heat that's better than no heat. The interpreter tells us we are paying for the coal and electricity with the money from payday. Anyway, feeling clean is comforting; I always feel better when I'm clean. Now I have a friend on the outside and a couple on the inside. Maybe this will work.

This afternoon we listen to the German radio news broadcast coming from the large speakers outside. The prisoners who understand the language explain the contents to the rest of us. The news goes on about the German Army's successful Ardennes offensive. It describes the German march through Luxembourg and Belgium all the way to Antwerp and the thousands of American and English captives taken. The weapons and matériel taken from the Allies greatly weakens any possibility of retaliation. They say this offensive will ensure the German victory.

This evening our interpreter tells us that the German news is manufactured for the ears of the German people and is a hoax. The Allies have stopped the German offensive and have captured, killed, or wounded the bulk of the German manpower. The Allies are on the offensive again, headed for Berlin and the end of the war.

"Soon the British POW force will arrive here from Poland. The Russian advance forced the Germans to move these prisoners." He adds, "They are bringing a crystal radio with them which will enable us to listen to the BBC news broadcast. When this is set up, I will visit each barracks and give a summary of the news and the locations of the American troops. We will keep you informed of how close the Americans are to this camp. We all want to know when we can leave here."

It's the end of January. I'm walking back with the detail from the kitchen with my food bucket under my field jacket. The German guard is the one we all have grown to like. He proudly wears his commendation ribbons from World War I on his sergeant's uniform. He is nice to us when he is on barracks duty. Some of the German-speaking prisoners speak with him and exchange pictures of loved ones. He looks like everyone's grandpa. He wears the insignia of a master sergeant. In the German Army, lower-ranked noncoms salute the upper ranks. When they salute, they do it properly, with a snap. He points to me and says something in German that I don't understand.

I think, *Oh, no, he's going to confiscate my food.* Simon warned me about this.

The man next to me says, "He's telling you to carry your bucket outside your coat, you're spilling it all over yourself." He adds, "He says you don't have to hide it."

I say to both of them, "Thank you."

I guess my food smuggling is no longer a secret. I hope this doesn't jeopardize the project. I thank the German master sergeant and give him a big smile. He returns it. The German soldiers are friendlier than the German civilians. Simon was right.

We halt for a work detail to pass, a detail of French Africans, big, happy-looking men. A pushcart is coming from the other direction, loaded with potatoes. A prisoner is pushing it accompanied by a guard. As the work detail passes the pushcart, a huge black man reaches over into the cart. The guard sees this and raises his rifle and strikes the black man on the shoulder. The black man gives the guard a big toothy smile, picks up a potato, looks him straight in the eye, and takes a healthy bite. The detail and the pushcart continue on their opposite ways. I bet that African would like to get his hands around the throat of that German guard.

If I were a general, I would give that African a medal for raising morale. After seeing what that man did, I feel as if my feet have been lifted off the ground. What a feeling of self-esteem. The hell with these bastards; now I know we will make it.

Today the scuttlebutt is flying: an American prisoner has been going over the fence each night. He actually crawls over the top of the gate and comes down across the street into the French compound. He carries with him watches, gold fountain pens, and rings. He gets these from American prisoners who want to exchange them for bread or cigarettes. A cigarette is worth two dollars, American; a slice of bread, the same. The American Army Post Exchange sells cigarettes at seven cents a pack and a loaf of bread is eight cents; we are looking at real inflation. This is my first lesson in the law of supply and demand, and it's a tough one. We hear that the black marketer has disappeared. He may have escaped the camp, carrying with him the profit from his enterprise. Silently we all wish him well; anyone who beats the system is a hero in our eyes.

This morning I'm visiting some new friends from the 9th Division in the next barracks. I'm sitting on the top bunk with my feet hanging down, balancing myself by holding on to the bunk edge with both hands. We're in the middle of a conversation when I hear this loud noise. It sounds like wood cracking. At that same moment I hear a plane roar over the top of the barracks. We hit the floor and we all lay flat. We hear the plane and we hear a machine gun firing.

"What the hell is that?"

"Look at the bunk where you were sitting."

I look up. A number of holes and splintered wood are next to where I had been sitting and where my hands had been on the top of the bunk. Holes are in the ceiling where the .50-caliber bullets came through the roof, through the bunk, and into the wall. I'm sitting on the floor and staring at those holes. It's unbelievable. How did they miss me? My friends run outside to see what's happening. I slowly rise and follow them. My knees are weak; I stumble out the door.

They are outside looking up with big grins on their faces. When I see it, I am grinning also. A P-38 American fighter plane is making a wide long swoop in the sky. The German machine gunner in the guard tower is tracking him and firing. What a mistake he is making. Since there are no tracer bullets from the German machine gun, we can't see the results. The P-38 comes in low and straight, with all his firepower pouring into that guard tower.

The tower disintegrates as if a bomb had hit it. It is gone. We yell and cheer. It is one for our side. We look around. We have lots of company. Every one is cheering. What a feeling! It is wonderful, just what we all need.

The plane makes one more pass over the spot where the guard tower had been; the pilot waggles his wings and is gone. What a sight to see; it's one for the good guys.

Early November, Huertgen Forest

I was in my foxhole, and the noise of explosions turned my attention to the open space in the tree branches. Through this open space in the trees I saw the sky full of P-47s dive-bombing. The beautiful sky was perfectly clear with a few white clouds; it must have been an excellent day for the fliers. They were bombing the town of Schmidt. This town on the mountaintop had been taken by the Americans, retaken by the Germans, then by the Americans. It was a focal point in the Huertgen Forest, evidently of great value to both sides.

The day was cold, the air was crisp, and the sound of the bombing was loud. I could not see the town from this position, but I could tell where it was from the rising smoke.

There were no German planes or antiaircraft offering resistance; the fliers must have had a turkey shoot. I sure envied those pilots, fighting in a clean uniform with a clean shave and their hair combed. When their bombs were gone, they turned around and flew home to a nice hot meal served inside a dining hall with heat. They might even have a date tonight. It was lonesome out there in the middle of nowhere. I wasn't going anywhere. Hopefully, if they returned tomorrow, I'd still be here. It was a good feeling knowing we had planes in the sky. Those pilots were lucky they didn't have to spend the night here.

I wish I could go back with them.

Ziegenhain, Germany

That night we all eagerly await the interpreter and the nightly news. He walks in without a guard and with a big grin on his face. He's good.

"I guess you all want to know about the plane."

We all shout, "Yes!"

"First of all," he says, "we have had some underground communication. We planned to lay panels in the field to indicate to the P-38 pilot how many Americans are here. You may have noticed there were workers in the field today. They were laying colored cloth panels for that plane to read. These panels had been prepared for today. There was no intention for the plane to fire on the camp, as that is against the Geneva Convention. When the guard fired on the plane, he broke the rules, as prison camps are out of bounds. We all saw the results. The plane waggled its wings to let us know he received the message. Now our troops know where we are and how many of us are here.

"Last night the British arrived. They are in their compound. They brought with them a crystal radio set that we have set up to receive the news from the British Broadcasting Corporation. It's working and we owe much to our friends for this. They broke the set down into the smallest components to be carried by individual men. When a man went down on the march, his component was turned over to another. All those on the march from Poland did not make it. It's a long way to walk and they're in bad shape from the trip. You won't see any British; they are isolated in their own compound. If you happen to meet one, thank him for the radio.

"The artillery we are hearing to the northwest is German. As the sound moves closer to us, we will hear the American guns moving east. That will indicate the American advance. I'll return tomorrow night with a blackboard and illustrate the American and German lines."

With that, he leaves. We all agree he is doing a tremendous job and we are grateful. I am awakened in the middle of the night by the yelling of the first sergeant who bunked across from me.

"The bastards stole my bread," he shouted.

"Who stole your bread?"

"I had bread inside my field-jacket pocket and rolled up; I use it as a pillow."

"You mean someone stole it from under your head?"

"Yes," he says. "All these guys are noncoms from the same outfit. We're all buddies."

"Some buddies," I say.

"The hell with them, I'm not a nursemaid to them anymore."

I thought anyone with that much talent should be able to figure a way out of here. Imagine, stealing that bread from under a guy's head while he's asleep. What will they think of next?

It is February and the prisoners are becoming testier with cabin fever. The Germans picked up the disappeared black marketer one day after his escape. He has been in solitary since. Two more are reported to have gone over the fence. The black-market business is flourishing. There are middlemen, end men, and men like me who just receive goods from the owner and pass them to the middleman, who passes them to a former supply sergeant. He then passes them to the buyer.

The business is easier now; the items are sold to the German guards, so no one goes over the fence. It is straightforward black marketing and no one loses. Everyone is paid his share and there are no complaints. The man who is running this operation must be planning to go home with bundles of cash. He does business with the French and the French have the access. Some French are permitted to walk to town and walk back again. The French prisoners and the German guards supply the black-market bread and cigarettes. The French I have seen wear clean, pressed uniforms and have their hair cut. The master sergeant guard tells me they have been here so long they consider it home. "They will never run away," he said.

He went on, "The Russians are different. They are wild and unruly and we watch them carefully because they don't like us. Same way with the Africans; they would kill us when they have the opportunity." Seems to be a nice, friendly group. The hostility is subdued so far.

Two prisoners are having a loud argument and now they are swinging at each other. One takes a good swing, misses, and falls on the floor, while the other jumps on top of him and rolls over on his back. We laugh; they look like Laurel and Hardy, except both are skinny. It's ridiculous; they both are so weak they couldn't beat up a pussycat. I notice one of my friends' clothes are hanging on him.

"Your pants are drooping."

He says, "You're getting thin too; look at your shirt." He is right.

Some of the prisoners who are naturally thin look like scarecrows. "I bet I could read the newspaper through that skinny one."

I walk outside by myself, thinking of the day in the Huertgen Forest when we went up on the line to relieve the 9th Division.

23 October 1944, the Huertgen Forest

We were located about a hundred yards behind the front line near Elsenborn. Any minute we would be going up on the line; the waiting was over. This is what we had been trained for; this is what we were dreading. Four of us were infantry replacements, referred to as cannon fodder. We were only a few of the thousands who would replace the casualties that were headed for the hospitals and cemeteries. The waiting was murder; my stomach was talking to me and I wanted to scream, Let's get it over with.

Which of the four of us would get it the first day, the first hour? Who would be killed outright? Which body would be torn apart? Who would get the million-dollar wound and go home in one piece?

We looked at one another in silence then turned away; no one had anything to say, and no one wanted to look cowardly. I was condemned to my fate. I was trying to be calm and collected. The apprehension was growing; I could smell it. My hands had begun to sweat. Is this the feeling of a man waiting to be hanged? I'm going to die, I think. The other eight soldiers of this squad were equally quiet; at least they knew what was ahead. They were combat veterans who made up the balance of the 2nd Squad, 2nd Platoon, I Company, 110th Regimental Combat Team, 28th Infantry Division.

Four of their buddies were gone. Would they welcome the four of us as part of the team or would we have to prove ourselves? Would they help us or would they let us hang ourselves? Can we four fill the gap? Did we have the guts for this job? I was determined to do my best, but I didn't know how I would react when the time came. I had never killed a man before.

"Hit it! We're going up on the line," said the platoon sergeant.

We all came out of our foxholes.

"Over here, Second Squad," yelled the squad leader. Eleven of us lined up behind this scraggly-looking old man. He was the squad leader. He sounded like a hillbilly, he looked like a hillbilly, and yes, he was a hillbilly. At second look he really wasn't old at all; he just seemed that way.

We were new recruits, having no idea what we were supposed to do next. I had been on a training cadre that taught infantry basic and even I was confused. We were heading into what we all were afraid of: war. "Move out," the squad leader shouted. And we did, leaving the peaceful area of hot chow and safe foxholes.

We were twelve, and alone in the woods. I was next to the end. The assistant squad leader was behind me. We carried our rifles at port; they were locked and loaded. I was stiff and rigid. I was petrified.

"This is it," said the man in front of me. "Keep your eyes open."

Mine were coming out of my head as I followed the man in front of me. I wondered if he was as scared as I was. Maybe the veterans didn't feel this way. Four of us were brand-new; the others had seen some combat. No one was talking as we started walking through the trees. The soft ground grabbed my boots as I made my way through the trees. This forest seemed so peaceful and quiet with its tall proud pines. I stretched my neck and saw just a bit of blue sky peeking down at us.

Then it began.

A tremendous noise like an express train, followed by a god-awful crash. Trees began breaking up, trunks and branches split and fell on top of me. Shells screamed and exploded; the noise was deafening. The world was exploding and I was about to die.

I hit the ground fast by instinct; no one was in sight. How did the Germans know where we were? We were in the wrong place. My face was buried under a fallen tree trunk. I was as tight as I could be under and behind this tree trunk. I forgot the four grenades hanging from my jacket pockets. I was waiting for the shell that would get me; it was just a question of which one.

More shells shrieked into us and exploded on the ground where the trees once stood. My tree didn't provide that much cover, too much of me was sticking out. I was going to be killed. Should it happen so soon? I had wanted to dig a hole under this tree and hide, but no one could have helped me. The shelling hadn't stopped, but it seemed to be moving away from us.

On my left and behind me, screams of "Medic!" scorched my ears. Was someone helping them? As I raised my head a few inches to look around, it seemed a giant monster had just walked through here destroying everything in its path. Split and broken trees looked helpless. Seventy-foot trees were now four-foot sticks coming up out of the ground. Pine branches and tree limbs were all over the place; it seemed sacrilegious. Splintered, bare tree trunks looked like white human bones. Maybe they were. What if one of those shells had hit me instead of a tree?

All at once it was quiet again. My mouth was dry.

I spotted the squad leader. He was standing up, leaning on his rifle and spitting chewing tobacco. Unbelievable. He looked like Daniel Boone. He looked as if he had been standing there all through this. He looked as if he belonged here. I slowly got to my feet and felt a great admiration for this man. He looked as if he were waiting for something, a true leader. He hadn't given a damn about the shelling, or anything else for that matter. I felt sheepish for hiding under that log. He might have thought I was a coward. I was scared, but I was not a coward. As I got myself together, I realized I had to do this, and I was going to do it right. I was going to learn from this hillbilly.

It was then I smelled the incenselike aroma of the pine in this cathedral-like setting. The soft quiet seemed to honor what was happening here today. My helmet was on straight, my four hand grenades were in place, my rifle wasn't dirty, and I hadn't shit in my pants. I was ready.

We began walking again, single file. When I was in the Boy Scouts, we used to walk single file through the woods. I wondered if the German

152

Boy Scouts ever walked on this path. By this time they would be soldiers like me, and there we were, trying to kill one another. We didn't learn this in the Boy Scouts. No one up ahead had fired his weapon. I hadn't heard anything, it was deathly quiet. There were no Germans to shoot at. That was fine with me. But both German and American weapons and helmets were lying around. I saw too many M1 rifles. That's what the sergeant meant about picking up a rifle when mine became too dirty to use. Casualties had been removed and the bodies must have been taken away yesterday. I didn't think they would do it at night. There must have been an awful fight here yesterday.

"Stop here and rest," the squad leader said.

American soldiers were coming in our direction. They were coming from the direction we were headed. I leaned against the tree with my rifle butt on the ground. Water from the canteen tasted good going down.

One soldier said to me, "Man, are we glad to see you."

"You are?"

"You're relieving our division from the line."

"Good luck," said another. They looked tired and filthy; most of them had beards. One stopped for a cigarette offered by one of our squad. I guess they didn't have to shave on the front line. They were from the 9th Division.

As we started up again, walking forward, more relieved troops passed. We moved closer to our destination and I was beginning to get a feel for what was going on. The terrain looked the same: ration and ammunition boxes, helmets and weapons from both armies. I wondered, Where are the soldiers that were in those helmets?

Passing over a firebreak, I saw a demolished log emplacement, empty. I didn't know if it was one of theirs or one of ours. It looked like a miniature log fort without a roof. Three-quarters of it was below the ground. Engineers must have built it. The logs were twelve inches thick and looked as if they had been blasted by a cannon, probably from a large tank. I smelled the smoldering, charred, and splintered structure. It was empty and looked abused and discarded.

A disabled tank was up ahead with a broken tread and the top blown off, sitting just off the firebreak. Someone had a bad time here. There were a few more weapons on the ground as we continued on this trail. Farther on, the men from Grave Registration were moving the bloated bodies of German soldiers. What a god-awful sight. Why didn't they just make this into a cemetery? It remained quiet as we continued through the broken trees toward the front line. This was the beginning.

Ziegenhain, Germany

I have a problem. There are enough prisoners to return the food tubs tonight. Two of them are grinning at each other. One says to me, "We don't need you tonight, we can handle the tubs." This means they are trying to cut in on my smuggled food from Simon. This means we won't have our extra food ration tonight. Our food operation has been successful now for three weeks and it's about to change.

I wait for their return. They have no German mess kit with food, so I ignore them for the present. Tomorrow I will alert Simon and see what can be done. My friends gather around as I show them a cigarette I earned today by selling a prisoner's gold pen to the black-market man for six American cigarettes. My cut is one cigarette, so we decide to remove the tobacco and roll it into two cigarettes.

None of us are smokers; we do this in the hope that the smoke will help soften our hunger pains. It has been an eternity since any of us has had a decent meal and we wonder if it's possible that we will starve to death. The cigarette tastes terrible; it's making me dizzy. We take turns taking a drag until it's all gone. The interpreter has not come tonight and we worry that something may have happened to him. Maybe the Germans found the crystal set. We lost the interpreter at Bad Orb. Lights out.

The next morning I decide to speak with Simon about my tub problem. I walk out the door into the barracks yard and head toward the fence separating our barracks from the mess hall. There is no one anywhere, so I stand by the fence and call Simon by name. I'm calling Simon for the second time when I feel something hard and small pressing against my right temple just above my right ear. Because I have an idea what it is, I don't move.

I freeze and slowly roll my eyeballs to the right. The something hard and small is now pressing harder. Out of the corner of my eye I see it's just what I am afraid it is. It's a German pistol. Holding the pistol is a German hand, on the end of a German arm. It's that bastard German civilian guard who hit me with his rifle butt. He knows who I am and he knows I recognize him.

I continue to freeze. He cocks the hammer. I stiffen. It sounds like an echo chamber inside my head. Is this the last sound I am going to hear? I hold my breath and wait. The hammer clicks again. I know what comes next. I think, Jesus, he's going to blow out my brains. We have been told the fence is off-limits to all prisoners.

I guess this gives him reason to shoot me. I turn my head slowly, feeling the gun pressed hard against my temple. If he's going to kill me, I'm going to watch him do it. I look him in the eye with hatred. My fear is gone. I feel disgust for this son of a bitch. I want to get my hands on his throat. I'll snap his neck like a stick. He looks to be about sixty. He's ugly and he has me. I can't move.

We are eye to eye. Neither of us flinches. My lips are quivering. He slowly withdraws the pistol from my head, but he does not release the hammer. He begins yelling in German. I can't understand him, but I know what he means. I'm shaking all over. I want to grab him. He uses the gun to prod me away from the fence. The gun remains cocked.

Looking at him, I turn slowly away from the fence and begin walking toward the barracks. I figure he will not shoot me now, in the back. I get to the barracks door and slowly turn. He's still there with the pistol in his hand. I turn farther and look at him. I'm thinking, I know hatred now.

Back in the barracks, I relate all this to my three comrades.

"What are you going to do?" asks Pete.

"I know exactly what I'm going to do the minute we are released," I answer. "I'm going to strangle the son of a bitch as soon as I find him, which shouldn't be difficult."

The following day we have some amateur entertainment. One prisoner tells jokes, and once he gets rolling, he has everyone howling and laughing. He tells us he was a nightclub comedian before he was drafted and we tell him how lucky he is to find a home in the army, he would have starved as a comedian.

He answers, "But I'm starving right here."

That brings a sober gloom over the group. Next we have a tenor sing some songs. He is also very good. When he sings about his sweetheart, it brings some deep thoughts to most of the men. Since I don't have a sweetheart, it doesn't bother me. I'm glad I don't have a wife or a sweetheart. The married men talk about their wives as if each were the Virgin Mary. Some worry that their wives may be unfaithful. To me, it's a sad subject. We all show our appreciation to the tenor.

After the group songs are over, we have some prayer. A chaplain's assistant leads us in prayer and asks for guidance and patience. He asks that we all come safely through this ordeal and that we forgive our captors. I don't tell him I'm going to kill one of mine. I decide to say a rosary each day. I don't have a rosary, but I remember the sequence from my Catholic school days.

That night the interpreter shows up. "Let me have your attention. I brought a blackboard to illustrate the war situation." With that, he draws in white chalk the current positions of both the Germans and the Americans. We all murmur our approval.

"Here is the front and how it pertains to us. Here are our troops; this is where they were two days ago, where they are now, and this is where they're headed. We are pushing the Germans in this direction. The Russians are in Poland and they are moving fast to the west. This movement is favorable to our release. You may have heard the artillery this morning; that was ours, not the Germans'. When you listen carefully, you can tell the difference. You'll continue to hear American artillery as it moves closer. Our troops are pushing hard.

"This area here is being swept by Patton's Third Army. All of us in this room are from the First Army. The Third Army is armored. The Third Army is making excellent progress toward this area." He goes on, "We have a number of men down with dysentery; some are in the infirmary. When the weather turns warm, the danger of dysentery will increase. This is serious in our condition, so keep all of your eating utensils as clean as possible. Our near-starvation diet has kept us weak, so we're susceptible to any type of disease. If our troops continue to advance, we may be out of here by the end of March. We have to stay alive and wait."

This was February 28; we had been here almost two months.

"What are you going to do about Simon?" asks Pete.

"You can't go near that fence," adds John. "That guard has his eye on you."

"I have an idea that may work, I'll let you know how it comes out," I answer. I figure there is no point in everyone worrying.

Just then the barracks leader breaks in with an announcement. "The camp commandant has offered us a work detail, volunteers to work on a bombed-out railroad section. The pay is extra food for those that go. This is our first detail, it will be one full day with picks and shovels."

The prisoner who spent one month in solitary for his failed escape says, "Don't go if you plan to escape. They will find you and bring you back. Solitary is no good."

I decide it sounds too dangerous. Since the American planes bombed the railroad tracks once, they could do it a second time while our detail is there working. We all pass on the detail. So far there have been three escapes and all three men have been returned and stuck in solitary. They simply went out through the fences at night. They were brought back through the front gate, and then put into solitary.

The next day the detail leaves. My ugly guard goes with them. At dusk, I approach the fence and wait until Simon comes out on the porch.

"Where have you been?" he asks. After I explain my problem, he volunteers an answer. "Come to the fence tomorrow at dusk and I'll walk over and hand you the mess kit. By that time it will be dark. That guard only works during the day. The next night you can return the empty mess kit."

This is the way we set it up, and it works well. Simon brings the loaded mess kit to the fence at just about dark. The next night I toss the empty mess kit over the fence to him. If for some reason he can't make a pass, I wait by the fence for only ten minutes, as we are forbidden to be outside after dark. If there is a guard detail in the street, we call it off. A few times I cut it a little close, but I am never caught. We don't always connect, but what food we receive helps. None of us catch dysentery.

We silently bless Simon.

---

4 November, Huertgen Forest

Last night the Germans counterattacked again. The same routine: they came out of the trees blasting. We couldn't see them, but we knew they were all over the place. I kept firing my rifle at the noise of their weapons. After a while it stopped and it was quiet. The old-timers told me the Germans did this to test the strength of our position. I wondered if I would get to be an old-timer.

The medics made the rounds tending the wounded. I don't know what we would do without the medics. When they hear a wounded man yell, they take off in his direction. They even work in this utter darkness. The volunteers then help get the wounded back to the aid station. How they can find anything in this darkness is beyond me. Some have wandered off into the darkness never to return. We all carry a pack of sulfa powder and bandages on our belts. This is to cover an open wound for others or ourselves. We use it until the medic arrives.

The black night was becoming a shade of gray as the trees came into focus and objects were taking shape. The silence was comforting as the green world awoke. The snow was peaceful; it made a beautiful scene. The war seemed to have gone away. I saw no Germans in front of me. Somewhere the sun was shining, but it didn't penetrate this graveyard-like silence in the forest. The brutal dark had gone. If it could only stay this way. Could today be Sunday?

"Okay, we're moving out." So much for tranquillity. The sergeant had a voice of doom.

This morning I crawled out of my foxhole. Other men were slowly staggering out of theirs. My body was stiff and sore, my back ached; something must have died in my mouth. It felt good to stand up and stretch. Now where the hell are we going? I wondered.

We walked back to the rear until we hit a road. It was a fairly typical dirt road, not very wide. We walked in single columns on both sides of this road, and I noticed that two of our squad were missing. This meant they were hit during the night. We were now three men short.

The road wound uphill. We marched the standard fifty minutes, then broke for ten.

I was wearing my overcoat over my fatigue jacket, pants, and long underwear, with my GI scarf around my neck. They helped in this cold, as did my GI gloves. I didn't even notice the weight of my field pack anymore; it had become part of me. Now it was the clothes on my back, rations, weapons, ammunition, and a blanket. My rifle was slung over my right shoulder with the muzzle pointed down, as it was beginning to drizzle. The rifle didn't seem as heavy in this position; the steel helmet never seemed heavy. It was the only body protection I had.

The road was getting muddier and longer and longer. The day was cold, wet, and dreary; then the water had begun to drip from the trees. Tall fir trees covered the road like an umbrella, only this umbrella leaked. Water was running off my helmet onto the back of my neck.

Snow on the ground was virgin white covering the road and the ground among the trees. No fighting or shelling here since it snowed yesterday as the trees were all intact. As I followed the back of the man ahead, it occurred to me that I didn't know what he looked like from the front. We had all been isolated in our individual foxholes; I didn't know any of these men.

The road was turning to solid mud; it was all over my shoes. What *the hell, I'd been wet for so long I didn't remember when I had been dry. My head was stuffed with the cold I've had for a month. This was a miserable existence and it was time for a break. We pulled off the road, headed into the trees, then stopped for our break. I left my knapsack on my back; it was too difficult to remove over my wet overcoat, so I leaned back against a tree. It felt good to stretch out. I wished I could sit here until the war was over. The ground cover was a mixture of white and brown mush. The rain was making little rivers in the snow.*

This was when we heard the news.

"We will form our skirmish lines here in the trees, before we begin the assault," came from our company commander.

I murmured, "Sweet Christ, just what we need."

"We will spread out, about three yards apart, and walk up this hill. We have been assigned the task of taking the town of Schmidt. It lies at the top of this rise.

"This rise," he continued, "is a completely bare field with no trees, no gullies, no fence, nothing. Nothing between us and the krauts at the top of the hill."

It was more like a mountain. Infantrymen were trained to find cover, no matter where they were. Nothing means no cover, nowhere to hide from the enemy.

I said to the man next to me, "This is crazy; they'll mow us down like wheat in a threshing machine."

He looked at me and said, "Yep."

I looked up the hill; the top was at least a half mile high.

The sergeant said, "Get ready to move, check your ammunition."

"The krauts are sitting up there watching us. They can't believe we're going to charge up the hill, right into their guns."

"Who is the idiot that came up with this one?" came from the back. A few hundred men were going to storm this hill.

"We'll all be killed," said a voice.

We came out of the trees into the open on lock and load; now we unlocked, ready to fire. Everyone was checking his bayonet, grenades, and ammunition.

"This is going to be bad," said the man next to me.

"Good luck," I croaked. My mouth was dry. I was tense. Now we all were silently making peace with our Maker.

Some were fixing bayonets. Although I taught bayonet in infantry basic, I didn't like it; I wanted the rifle free to fire. If I get close enough to use it, I'll insert it then.

This was why infantrymen were referred to as cannon fodder. This was a job to do. To the left and right, the troops were spread out as far as I could see. It was too far for us to run; we had to walk to the top of this hill, straight into the heart of the enemy.

I said to the next man, "What the hell are we supposed to shoot at, there's no one in sight."

"We should have artillery cover for this, but we don't."

We received orders to go forward.

"Wait," said our squad leader, "it's been called off." It was mass confusion as we all hurried back to the cover of the trees. "The assault has been called off," he said. "We are moving this way through the woods. Follow me out of here."

What a feeling of relief. The many prayers were answered.

I was following the assistant squad leader. I guess he didn't want to be last in line in case we were hit from the rear. What a jerk. I said to myself, This guy is more scared than I am. We proceeded down a gully, deeper into the woods. Gray snow was turning to slush and the ground was softening. It was tough going through the pine trees and heavy brush. I was holding my rifle higher to avoid the snags. Bushes and tree limbs grabbed me as if they didn't like this intrusion.

Incoming fire began and I hit the dirt. The assistant squad leader screamed, then went down. We had walked right into it.

"Medic!" He was hit. He was in the position I should have been in. The krauts were on the side of the opposite slope. They were firing rifles and burp guns. The burp guns have an incredible high, fast pitch. There was no mistaking this weapon. It sprayed bullets all over the place.

I was now behind a fallen tree trunk returning fire. Germans were in some type of enclosure on that slope; I could just barely see them. I was zeroing in on what looked like a German helmet. I couldn't see well enough to know that I was hitting what was out there, but I was sure trying. This place was dark, the trees and foliage were thick. The Germans must have been waiting for us to walk into their field of fire. This might have been a pillbox. The only way out of here was to kill every one of them.

More cries for the medic came from my left. I didn't turn around, I kept firing. This was no time for thinking, only firing at what was out there with as much accuracy as possible.

The krauts were giving us trouble. More rifles were firing from my right and the firing picked up on the left. The man across from me screamed; he was hit. It looked like these krauts knew what they were doing. We all were pumping in lots of firepower.

Another cry for the medic to my left. We were going down fast here. The krauts were too far away for hand grenades. I inserted another clip into my rifle and continued to fire, the more the better. We were losing this battle. Those bastards were tough.

The explosion ended the fight. It must have been a bazooka shell. There was nothing coming out of the kraut position but smoke. It was over, just as quick as it started. Someone did a real job with that bazooka. It couldn't have been a tank or a 37mm antitank gun; the foliage here was too dense.

I inserted a new clip into my rifle. My rifle smelled and the barrel was hot. I had no idea how long I had been firing. Time seemed to have stopped. These things always ended like they began: instantaneous. Lots of men went down here. This brush was so thick I saw only one poor bastard with the blood leaking out of him like oil pouring out of a transmission. I felt sorry for him and I didn't even know him. The pain must have been terrible, the way he was screaming. A medic was over him. The wounded thank God for the medics.

What was left of us got up and started to form a group. Regrouped, we proceeded down the gully. The medics were left behind with the wounded. I guessed the chaplain would come for those who didn't make it. I saw the assistant squad leader lying there with a medic; he wasn't moving. He might be dead. That could have been me if he had been in his proper position. Our squad was getting smaller. We had lost two more today.

I had no idea where we were or where we were going, but I was relieved we didn't have to assault that hill to take the town of Schmidt. We came out of the woods and began to move up a mountain road. The rain had stopped.

I checked my bandolier. I had used more ammunition than I figured in that last fight. I discarded the empty bandolier and checked the clips I had in my belt. I had five clips and two hand grenades, not much if the krauts hit us again. I must have used those other two grenades last night. Sometimes my reaction was quicker than my brain. I guessed I was learning my trade. Lack of ammo shouldn't be a problem; we always had plenty of that.

We came out of the woods into a bare area about three hundred yards from the next patch of woods, and stopped for a break. This was insane, out in the open with all these krauts around. We were told to dig in. This meant we were to dig foxholes for ourselves, here and now.

Through the trees came three American soldiers from the 1171st Engineer Combat Group. "Where are you guys going?" one of them, a tech sergeant, asked me. They looked just like we did, old and tired.

I replied, "*Who knows.*"

"*German tanks are down in that gully, we saw them last night and came up here to get away from them. We were supposed to be building a bridge for our tanks and the krauts show up. I'm a bridge builder not a dogface. It's your job to fight them, not mine. We lost some Weasels [tracked vehicles] down there and we lost some engineers. You'd better watch where you're going.*"

Our platoon sergeant said, "Dig those holes deep enough so you're not squashed when the Tiger tanks run over you."

I said to him, "What the hell are we doing out here in the open?"

"*Just follow the orders.*"

When we dug a foxhole, it was a two-man job. One man carried a small pick and the other man had a small shovel in the pack he carried on his back. A pick or a shovel was standard gear and these tools were small enough so a soldier could lie down on his side and dig while under enemy fire. The sergeant was correct; sergeants usually are. These tools were not meant to be used in the conventional manner, from a standing position; they were too small.

Since we were not under enemy fire, we knelt down and attempted to dig a hole at least three feet deep, six feet long, and three feet wide. When under enemy fire, most soldiers would dig a shallow depression to fit their body, just below the level of the ground. This offered some protection from small-arms fire. When an enemy tank rolled over this depression, there was no protection from being crushed to death. There was also no protection from the deadly tree bursts.

The ground is frozen hard. "It's impossible," I said to my buddy. "The hell with it; if the tanks come, I'm heading for those woods."

"*I'm with you.*"

So we sat down and had some K rations and water from the canteen. Five more combat engineers joined us; it was beginning to look like a picnic. We had been there for about half an hour when we got the command to move out. We proceeded up the mountain road. So much for digging the foxhole.

We heard the small-arms fire from the gully, then the loud boom of the tanks. Someone was catching it in that gully and on the far mountain slope. Through the trees on the other mountain, we could see a disabled American vehicle of some sort. There was another one.

They were in trouble. I was too far away to hear the screams of the men.

What were they doing in these dense woods? We were now in the cover of the woods, near the top of the mountain. American casualties were lying on the ground being tended by our medics where they lay. Being in the front, they must have run into more Germans before we caught up with them.

The German 88 shelling began blasting into the trees. The tree bursts were butchering those below. The noise was unbearable; I wanted to scream. We were in total confusion as we all scattered. We were getting our ass whipped. How come the Germans knew where we were and we didn't know where they were until we ran into them? They had the advantage and we were going to be wiped out.

I found an empty foxhole, rolled in, and buried myself in the hole. I heard a scream; a body fell in on top of me. Was it a kraut? It wasn't; it was a dogface. He was wounded in the leg. I cut open his pants and poured the sulfa from my pack all over the raw meat. He was in great pain. He had been hit just before he made it to this hole. I felt sorry for him, so I gave him some of my water. I yelled for the medic.

The medic stuck his head in the hole and said, "Give me enough room to give him some morphine." I crawled out of the hole and rolled under a tree. The shelling had stopped. There were cries all over the place for medics.

Were there no brains in this outfit?

Ziegenhain, Germany

I'm lying on my bunk with my leg hanging over the side when I feel a tug on my foot. This gets my attention fast and I sit up. A German soldier is standing there smiling at me.

A man close by says, "He's a paratrooper. He sees by your boots you're a paratrooper too."

I smile and say, "*Ja.*"

The soldier points to his noncommissioned officer stripes and says something. My interpreter says, "He's a sergeant. Are you?"

I hold four fingers against my sleeve and he nods with a smile. I feel so relieved that this is a friendly gesture, it makes my whole day. "Thanks," I tell the interpreter.

"You've made a friend, he respects you as a combat soldier," says my interpreter.

"Did you notice he has a bad leg?" As the German limped away I thought how decent it was of him to come over and talk to me. What a change from all the hatred we have here. When that German sergeant goes home, he'll take that limp with him. He'll have it the rest of his life. My father did.

The Battle of Aisne-Marne, Germany, 1917

Two American soldiers were in the burning barn. The German shelling had stopped and now was the time to get out. The first man found an opening the chickens used. He put his head down and began to wriggle through the small space. The sound that was like a pumpkin exploding was his head. The second man pulled the first away from the open space. Burning timbers were falling on them.

The second man, learning from this, went feetfirst, wiggling through the space. He had to get out. A tremendous pain shot into both his legs as he pushed himself free. He had been hit. A German sniper had shot both him and his companion. The bullet went through his right leg and was embedded in the left.

The medics found him fifty yards from the burned-out barn, where he had crawled and passed out. He spent one year in the military hospital and carried the limp the rest of his life. He went home with the Silver Star for valor and the Purple Heart for the wounds.

This second man was my father.

Ziegenhain, Germany

The railroad detail returns, after replacing the bombed-out railroad tracks. A GI tells us, "The civilian prisoners may have been Poles." American planes did come over and bomb the site, forcing the prisoners to take cover in the concrete culverts nearby.

Some civilians were hurt, but no Americans. There would be no American volunteers the next time.

It is "news time." The interpreter arrives and is accompanied by a captain in an American uniform. He sets up his blackboard and begins to talk. "This is Captain _____. He is from the _____ Airborne Division. He has been recently picked up by the Germans and brought to the closest POW camp," he states. "Since we're all noncoms, he will act as our leader. He and I will work together to give you representation with the camp commander. We will work together gathering as much information as possible pertaining to our release.

"Tonight's news is good," he continues, and begins to outline the battle lines of the German and American forces. He shows the 3rd Army advancing rapidly, taking thousands of German prisoners.

"The German Wehrmacht is made up of teenagers and old men. This Army is the last manpower they have; it's the bottom of the barrel. The Russians are advancing from the east and meeting resistance; the casualties are high." He then illustrates our position in relation to the 3rd Army's lead troops.

"We can now hear the American artillery and how each day it moves closer and closer. When the time comes, there will be a special attachment that will swing in here to rescue us. This is so we won't be caught up in the actual combat. The German Air Force is nonexistent, so we don't have a problem from the sky. Tomorrow the Swedish Red Cross will be here inspecting the camp's facilities. Red Cross boxes are in the camp warehouse; boxes will be distributed."

One box is for each man, not like the distribution on the train. Nothing can contain the happiness felt by each and every man in that barracks. We all roar our pleasure.

"We have to be as careful as we can about sanitation," he goes on. "There have been a number of deaths reported from dysentery. Fortunately, none of these have been Americans. We do have three men in the infirmary. The Germans are short on medical supplies and can offer little medical aid to the sick. Food and medicine are in short supply; don't look for help from either." He reports that he will return within the next few days with more news.

Frank, a staff sergeant from the 28th Division bunking next to me, says, "I was standing outside by the gate this afternoon. I saw two men, each lying in a wheelbarrow. They were dead. The German guard said they were headed to the graveyard. They had come from the hospital."

I say, "Simon's food has helped our condition; it should keep us alive until we get out of here, then I'm going to strangle that guard."

"Does the guy bother you that much to kill him?"

"He's my driving force. I think of him and his smirky smile. That son of a bitch isn't going to walk out of here."

The next morning the representatives from the Swedish Red Cross arrive in our barracks. The interpreter had us line up for distribution of the boxes. Sure enough, we all receive a box. A cry rises: "Those krauts stole our cigarettes."

I laugh and say to Frank, "The boxes have been opened and the cigarettes are missing."

"You can laugh," said Frank. "All we have to smoke are the cigarettes you bring from the black market." I have to admit my black-market activity had not been overly lucrative.

"I hope I'm out of here before I learn to smoke."

The Red Cross people ask us about the food, accommodations, and recreation. We tell them the truth. We have little of the first two and none of the third, but we have not been mistreated; we are cold and hungry and want to go home.

The Red Cross man tells me, "The German people are suffering without food, fuel, and medical supplies; the war has done terrible things to this country. The German Army receives most of what is available and that is not much. The end is near. Be good soldiers. These people will still be suffering long after you have gone."

With that, the inspection is over. The Swedes are nice men

and we welcome their friendliness. They could do nothing for us, but they do make sure we receive the food boxes. In the corner, a number of prisoners are already auctioning off some of the items from their Red Cross boxes. Yankee ingenuity.

I am sitting on my bunk eating some crackers and canned chicken. There is no way to describe how delightfully satisfying this is. I eat very slowly to make it last. It is so good.

"This is only the second time in almost three months I am eating something decent," says Pete.

"How can I go back to eating that lousy bread and warm water?" Frank adds.

I smile. "You'll eat it and love it."

"We do have Simon's food," I said.

And we all smile. I am thinking about another time when my mouth was full.

---

16 December, 4:00 P.M., Luxembourg

The telephone ring was from Pete at the foxhole to the left of the road. "We're in trouble: there's a German tank on top of our foxhole. What do we do?"

I had just stuffed my mouth with pancakes and strawberry jam, wrapped around bacon. I answered, "Keep perfectly quiet; if he knows you're there, he'll back up and blow you away. You're okay as long as he doesn't know you're there."

"You sound funny; are you okay? You're not wounded or anything, are you?" Pete asked.

I felt so damn guilty with my mouth full. "I'm fine, just be still until that tank moves."

The two of them kept perfectly quiet and the tank did move. I still felt sheepish.

Ziegenhain, Germany

It's mid-March. Each night we are shown the blackboard illustration of the front lines; each day the American artillery sound has moved eastward. The 3rd Army is moving fast, deeper into Germany. Time is crawling, but it's crawling toward the day of our release. The weather has grown warm; the snow has gone. Walking around the barracks, more and more of us look like scarecrows. Simon continues to provide the mess kit and so far I haven't been caught.

Yesterday I picked up a few more cigarettes that we share. Now we spend our time discussing how our release might take place. There are more men down with dysentery. They hide their problem so they are not forced to move to the hospital. No one wants to see the inside of that hospital. So far Frank, Pete, George, and I are well.

During the last week in March, the interpreter and the captain arrive but do not have the blackboard with them. They ask for volunteers to guard both barracks' doors and the latrine. There aren't any German guards around.

The interpreter begins, "We have something very serious to discuss tonight. The camp commandant has informed us of his orders from the high command. All prisoners except the Russians will be marched to Austria. The Americans, English, French, and the French Africans will remain in their own groups. All Russians remain here. The German camp guards will accompany this formation. We will remain in confinement in Austria until the war is over. We prisoners will be part of the peace negotiations. We are valuable property."

The room is buzzing with the reaction. A voice from the back says, "On the road, we outnumber the guards fifty to one."

"Exactly. We need volunteers to eliminate the guards; we are not going to Austria. We need to make homemade knives and other implements to carry out the plan. We will also have a signal so we can carry out the plan at precisely the same moment. We must take them all down at the same time on the first day of the march."

I look at the other three of our group and say, "Let's do it." They nod in agreement. Now we four have a plan.

The interpreter goes on: "We'll work out the logistics of how many volunteers are required and just how we will carry out this operation. I expect we'll be moving within a day or two. The American Army is getting close. This morning we heard small-arms fire in the distance. We'll talk tomorrow night. In the meanwhile, the captain and I will attempt to convince the commandant that the Americans are in no condition to march."

The interpreter and the captain leave, and we have something to think about.

The following day we are all busy making weapons from whatever we can scrounge. Some split wood with a six- or eight-inch point, some rip metal strips from the windows and grind the edge on concrete until it becomes a sharp point, some break up the metal stovepipe and make sharp, crude knives. There is no shortage of ingenuity here. We are soldiers once again and we mean business.

I decide to use a sharp sliver of glass with an ugly, mean point. I insert one of my gloves inside the other to make a handle. This baby is lethal. Whatever the weapon, it is to be used at very close range. We will be up against rifles, pistols, and submachine guns with live ammunition. None of the four of us has ever killed anyone like this.

"Let's go outside and check the sound of the artillery," says George.

Throughout the day I can hear the faraway booming of the American artillery. The German artillery sound of past days is no longer heard. Outside we find a springlike day. This is getting better and better.

"Maybe we won't make the march to Austria," I think out loud. The anticipation is building up like a pressure cooker and all the prisoners are talking about how and when.

"Simon told me his people were not told about the march. They've heard nothing from the Germans. But they're aware of the American advance," I say to Frank. "Simon's people will be glad to kill the Germans, but they need the opportunity."

The following night the interpreter and the captain appear again, as promised. It's dark. Again, there aren't any German guards. And again, we post our guards at the doors before the interpreter speaks.

"The plan has changed. The compounds are moving out tomorrow morning. The Russians and the Africans remain; the English, French, and Americans go. The three nationalities form on the soccer field. All prisoners will stay in formation and proceed to the main road. This is the beginning of our journey. Except for one thing: we are not going. The commandant will not believe we are too weak to march; therefore, we will prove it to him. This is what we are going to do."

The captain says, "We may be laying our ass on the line, but we've all done it before. Tomorrow morning we will assemble on the soccer field. The English and the French will be separated. Just after we are in formation, every third man falls to the ground and wails like he's sick. The others stay in formation but attempt to help the fallen men. We are putting on an act for the Germans. They probably won't believe it. Believe it or not, we will stall until the English and the French have left the field. We will continue to stall until they are all gone.

"Don't allow the German guards to keep you from your assignment. The Germans are scared to death the American troops will arrive before they get out of here. They're in a big hurry to leave. They're afraid to shoot us. Because of this, they won't waste much time harassing us to move. They're thinking about saving their own hides and they're afraid of capture. If we hold on, we can stay until our troops arrive. They're very near. If for some reason this doesn't work, we will go back to the first plan. Once we're on the road, we will kill the German guards. I'll see you all in the morning."

The two of them move on to the next barracks.

"We have a real morning ahead of us," says Pete. "This is going to be a real show. Do you think all these GIs have the guts to pull this off?"

"No," I answer, "but there will be enough of us to do it."

"The main thing," says George, "is to stall and stall until the Germans have to run for it. You can bet that commandant knows exactly where the American troops are."

"We have much at stake here and we have many things going for us," Frank says.

"Remember the machine gun at Bad Orb?" adds Pete.

We all agree it will be tough trying to get to sleep tonight.

It's morning. We have the morning chicory. Everything looks the same.

"*Raus,*" comes from the three German guards as they enter the barracks. And outside we go. No, today isn't the same as usual, but the weather is. It's an overcast sky and the temperature is mild. Today will be different. It is a day like the last time we were all ordered outside at Bad Orb. Today there is no machine gun.

I see the English and the French in formation across the field. The captain brings us to attention. This is the soccer field we never used. The actors begin to play their parts; Frank and I hit the ground while Pete and George act as if they're helping us. All throughout the formation American prisoners are going through the same routine, falling down and moaning.

The German officers are raising hell while the French and English prisoners are marching off the field. The German soldiers are telling us to get up and march. They are everywhere, poking their rifles into the ribs of those standing.

The Germans remove the captain and the interpreter. They are gone. We all continue the charade. It's mass confusion; the Germans act like they don't know what to do. We keep on with the moaning. More GIs are on the ground. Now two-thirds of the Americans are on the ground. Everyone wants to be a casualty.

The English and French are gone. The Germans are frantic. Now they're threatening to shoot us. Not one shot is fired. The captain was right; they're afraid to shoot us. It looks as if the great exodus has begun. We don't want to go. We continue the charade. Ten minutes go by, then twenty minutes; the German soldiers are leaving.

Thirty minutes go by; we are alone. We haven't planned the next part.

What *is* the next part?

The interpreter shows up. "Go back to the barracks and don't come out. The camp commandant took off last night. The officer in charge was going to shoot the captain and me this morning for our stalling. The Germans know it is all a fake. They made a bargain that we wouldn't be shot if all the Americans would march. The captain wouldn't agree.

"He told them if we were executed, the American Army would catch up with them. All the American prisoners would be witnesses. He advised the Germans to leave while they could, as the American Army would arrive tomorrow. They're gone now, but they left behind the civilian guards, armed with weapons. The Americans should arrive soon. Lay low."

The four of us start back toward the barracks. As we pass the outhouses, we can see American prisoners hiding in the bottom of the holes, in all that mess. The holes are all full of GIs, hiding for their lives. Some prisoners are hiding under bunks in the barracks and outside under the barracks themselves. Some have dug holes under the barracks and covered themselves with dirt. There are men hiding in every conceivable nook and cranny. These are the ones who were too scared to join the formation. I feel no empathy toward them. They're the ones who didn't have the guts to make it all work out.

They would have been useless if we had been forced to march with the French and British.

The four of us agree that the strong must carry the weak. It seems plan B might be successful. It's much simpler than plan A. I finger the sharp-pointed piece of glass in my pocket. I'll be using this on that guard.

Looking out the window of the barracks, I see that the civilian guards remain at the front gate. I wonder what is going through their minds. My adversary is around here somewhere. I decide to wait for the Americans before I look for him.

"Hello, Simon, what do you think about all of this?" I yell across the street.

He's standing on the porch of the kitchen with a big grin on his face. "It's time to go home," he answers. "Isn't it wonderful? After the Americans arrive, you must come and visit me."

"I certainly will."

"Don't forget the food at the fence tonight; it may be your last."

I agreed to meet him at dusk. We eat our regular food, then the mess-kit food from Simon. All the talk is about home and getting there.

"Tonight is a blessing compared to last night. I wasn't sure we could pull it off. I wonder how long it will be until we see some rescuers," says George.

"Maybe they'll show up tomorrow," Pete says. "One thing is for sure: we've seen the last of the German Army, unless they decide to use us as a human shield. That was something with the captain and the interpreter. They must have had a hot time while we were stalling the parade."

"Those two have been a blessing to all of us," I reply.

The man in the next bunk says, "Did you hear? The Russians broke out and went to Ziegenhain. They're sacking the town like animals. Some of them have come back with meat, potatoes, and anything else they can carry."

"They can have it. I just want to get out of here."

Pete says, "There's talk about jumping the civilian guards and taking over the camp."

"Then what do we do, pray for deliverance? That's stupid. I'm staying put, just like we were told."

We sleep easy that night.

We awaken in the morning to the sound of small-arms fire.

George gets up and looks outside. "It's coming from the woods."

We walk outside, and sure enough, those damn-fool krauts are having it out with the American Army. The woods are about a half mile behind the soccer field. We can't see any troops from either side, but they sure are going at it with machine guns and rifles.

"There are no guards in the guard towers," observes George.

"We only have the civilian guards now," adds Frank. We then hear the *whump* of American tank cannons. Then there is silence. "Looks like the Sherman tanks ended the party over there."

We walk out to the other side of the soccer field and begin yelling. "Maybe they'll hear us and come over," says Pete.

We look out and there are American tanks and armored infantry half-tracks coming down the road from Ziegenhain. Hallelujah! They are coming.

"They're here, they're here." The shouting greets us as we approach the barracks. An American tank is at the gate.

We all rush outside. And there it is. We all pile out of the barracks, into the street and through the gate. The tankers seem to be as happy to see us as we are to see them. The tankers are handing out cigarettes, cigars, K rations, and copies of the *Stars and Stripes*.

What a time. "It's over," I say. "What a relief."

"We knew about where you were located. It took a little time to find you, but you're safe now. The krauts are on the run," says one of the tankers.

"We're sure glad to see you."

We go back in the barracks to eat our K rations. They taste so good. The interpreter is speaking.

"Soon the trucks will arrive; they'll have some bread and

179

maybe some coffee for us. The important thing is, we will be leaving here tomorrow for a rest camp. Until then, stay inside the barracks. We will designate some temporary Military Police from the prisoners to keep everything safe. Do not wander around; some scared German civilian might shoot you. You are no longer prisoners of war; you are in the American Army. You will obey orders as always. You are all noncommissioned officers and will act accordingly. The Russians have violated the town of Ziegenhain. The civilians have shot some of them in defense of their homes and families. Thank the Lord we all came through this with only a few casualties."

Then he leaves. The four of us digest his words with great happiness. I know what I am going to do.

I go outside into the main street. An American prisoner is standing there with a rifle. He has a dark red armband on his sleeve.

"Where did you get the rifle?" I ask him.

"We confiscated the guards' rifles, just for MP duty, until we leave tomorrow."

"Does that armband give you the authority to get around in the camp?"

"Yes, why?"

"I have a friend I would like to visit in the African section. He smuggled food to me while we were here."

"Here," he says, offering his armband, "take mine, I'll get another from the tank."

"Thanks." I put on the armband and walk away.

It's late afternoon. I find the African compound and enter the first barracks.

As I open the door I see it's full of Africans. They are sitting on the floor. With the door closed, it is black as pitch except for the fire burning in the middle of the floor. I can just barely see the figures around the fire. A voice calls out, "Sergeant."

It's Simon. I throw my arms around him and hug him real good.

"It's so good to see you," I say.

"It's good to see you outside," he says. "Sit down and have something to eat."

He shoves some meat into my hand and I take a bite. I have no idea what it is, and I'm not going to ask him to tell me.

"Thank you."

We sit down and he explains who I am as he introduces his friends and comrades. They're wondering how they are going to get home. Simon tells me about his family and I tell him about my background. The other men are friendly; they speak French.

"Have you seen that guard?" Simon asks.

"No, but I'm going to look for him now."

"Don't do anything you will be sorry for later."

"I won't be sorry," I answer.

He is wearing a Middle Eastern red fez. "Lets trade hats," he suggests.

"Good idea." I give him my GI knit hat that I wear under my helmet. He gives me his fez. "Now I look like a South African dignitary." He laughs, then we exchange names and addresses. We both write on the stalag post card. Simon has learned to read and write English during his five years of internment. He speaks like an Englishman and I owe him so much. "I'll try to see you tomorrow before we leave," I add.

I open the door to leave. They are a roomful of African soldiers on their way home. I wonder if their barracks will burn down before morning. I'm sure the African soldiers don't care one way or another.

As I leave I see a rifle leaning against the wall. I pick it up. It's not loaded. I sling it over my shoulder. Now I look just like a temporary MP. I cut back through our compound and head for the soccer field. Where would that German guard be hiding? I can't shoot him even if I find bullets; it would make too much noise. I'll strangle him; that's what I figured on anyhow.

I walk through the compound next door and walk toward the rear. It's getting dark and hard to see. There is something over there in that wheelbarrow. It's him. He is stretched out on his back. He must be asleep. I reach over to grab him. I'm tensed. I'm going to do it right now. He has seen the last of this world.

He doesn't move. He is not asleep, he is not breathing. He's dead. His neck is at an odd angle. His neck is broken; someone has beaten me to it. I just realize what I almost did—kill another human being with my bare hands. How could I do such a thing? If I had arrived earlier, would I have done it?

I drop to one knee and give thanks that this violent act never came to pass. I am so relieved. I wonder about whoever has looked out for me through all this, who has now saved me again. I am so thankful I didn't kill that man. I am only twenty years of age; I would have carried the weight of it to my grave. I would have been ashamed. Just like I felt with the little bird.

I sit on the edge of the wheelbarrow next to the corpse and study the sky. The heavens are dark tonight. There has to be reason for all this. My body feels drained, my mind feels empty. If there is a God in heaven, I owe Him so much. A month ago, when I was saying my rosary, I made a vow. I said if I got out of this prison camp alive, I would never again ask for anything, nothing.

Slowly I get up and begin to walk. I'm shaken and I'm not sure where I am. This part of the camp is new to me. Then I hear the noise. It sounds like a party, a loud party. I head for the nearest building. The door is open; there is hell-raising going on here. It's the Russians. I swing the rifle from my shoulder and hang it over my back with the sling across my chest. In this manner no one can pull it away from me, just in case.

I walk through the door. The place is bedlam. It's a slaughter-house; it's a kitchen; no, it's a barracks. Tonight it's all three. Cooking fires are burning inside the barracks and outside, fed with wood from the bunks. Sides of meat are hanging from the ceiling, dropping blood all over the floor. Five of the Russians are sitting on the floor eating meat, potatoes, vegetables, and the works. They greet me with a hearty welcome, waving the meat and bottles they have in their hands. All of them are eating with their hands and drinking from the bottles. They are drunk but friendly.

A bottle is pushed into my hands. I know if I drink liquor in my condition, I'll pass out. I press the bottle to my mouth, but I don't swallow any liquid. It's some kind of whiskey. The stench from animal blood, human stink, whiskey, grease from the meat, and heavy smoke from the fires is overpowering. It's so dark in here I don't see anyone but this group. Their dark brown uni-forms are filthy and their black boots muddy. All have dark com-plexions, black hair, and Asian eyes. It's insane. They don't speak English and I don't speak Russian, but we all understand one another. We have one common enemy and now it is gone. We all are armed. They don't know I'm carrying an empty rifle. And they aren't going to find out. Some of them have pistols in their belts and others have rifles on their laps.

They look meaner than hell. I wonder how long they will stay friendly. I see some furniture and linens over on the bunks. This must be the crew that visited Ziegenhain. Rumor has it they brought back some women, but I don't see any. Two of them point to my armband and nod their heads up and down. Another points to my rifle and raises his eyebrows. They think I'm some kind of important person. The fez on my head gets their attention.

They may think I'm here on some kind of inspection. They know I'm an American. They can't see my rifle isn't loaded. It stays where it is. They also know about the American tank sitting at the gate. The short Russian with the shifty eyes on my left is slowly snaking his greasy fingers along the stock of his rifle toward the trigger. His eye is on my rifle and my eyes are on him. If my rifle were loaded, I would be getting set to shoot him. But it isn't. The others are watching both of us. Now is the time for me to get out of here.

I step back and they nod their heads again. The tall one reaches out; he hands me a side of lamb chops, a sack of potatoes, and a frying pan. It is obvious they'd rather I prepare my food somewhere else. This is exactly the idea I have. The sooner I leave, the better. That little bastard with the shifty eyes is bad news. As I prepare to leave they yell with big grins on their faces and wave the bottles. I have no idea what they are saying. Maybe it's "Up yours."

Outside, I shift all my items into position as I wonder, *Are they the Mongols of Genghis Khan?* Whatever they are, I'm damn glad to be out of there. No wonder the Germans are afraid of them; they look like cannibals. I've had a busy day. A visit to Africa, then Russia, and now home.

"Frank, get some wood. I brought home supper."

"Where in the world have you been?" he asks.

"Doing some shopping."

"Where did you get that hat and that rifle?"

"I'll tell you all about it; we're having fried potatoes and lamb chops."

Pete says, "We have white bread and it tastes like angel food cake, unbelievable."

We break up a bunk and build a fire outside and then cook the food in the frying pan. We eat the meat and potatoes right out of the pan with our fingers. It is delicious.

We gorge ourselves. Twenty minutes later, we throw up, all four of us, all of it. The three of them ask me about the guard. I tell them the truth. Much has happened tonight.

During the night, the 9th Armored arrives with the trucks. The next morning we leave for Le Havre, France. March 31, 1945. It's over.

EPILOGUE

On 7 November 1944, the war stopped. A two-hour cease-fire in the Hürtgenwald called by Günter Stüttgen, captain and physician of the 89th German Infantry Division, was approved by the high command. Both American and German soldiers were relieved from this three-day slaughter. During the cold, dark night, what remained of the original 220 men of I Company, 28th Infantry Division, dropped their weapons and felt their way through the trees, carrying the wounded on hastily made stretchers down this treacherous mountain to the Kall Bridge, where Dr. Stüttgen and American and German medics attended those on the stretchers and the walking wounded. German ambulances would take the wounded to the hospital. I was a stretcher bearer, naked with no weapon.

On 7 November 2004, an inauguration ceremony was held at the Kall site with a stone sculpture commemorating this humanitarian effort. Dr. Stüttgen had already received the highest humanitarian award from the American and German governments. The oil painting *A Time for Healing* illustrating those two hours hangs in the museum of the German National Guard headquarters. A copy hangs in Vossenack.

Many years have gone by. The names Frank, Pete, George, Red, Colonel, Bill, John, Tex, and Slim have been used to identify those wonderful soldiers who helped me through the Huertgen Forest, the Bulge, and prison camp. The years have gradually faded the faces until they have become obliterated. The names, also, have been swept away by time, but I will never forget them.

I wrote to Simon, but received no answer. I hope he made it home with his new hat; he deserved it.

The Army was wonderful. In Le Havre, we received everything we wanted: hot showers, clean clothes, a bed, and an open mess hall. We ate not when we were hungry, but to keep from getting hungry. I had lost forty-one pounds from my no-fat body. We were permitted to keep fruit and bread in our quarters, just to know it was there for us. Hunger is a terrible feeling. Our stomachs were small and our bodies weak. We were given a week in Paris before sailing for home. I met a girl with green hair, but I returned in three days. It was all too much.

We spent a week at Fort Dix, New Jersey. We were among the first POWs to return. We received special consideration; the *New York Times* raised hell about the fact that Fort Dix didn't have enough cigarettes for the repatriated Americans POWs, while the German prisoners interned there had all they wanted. It was a nice feeling that the American public was caring for us. On VE Day, I stood on the corner of Forty-second Street and Broadway in New York City, handing out real German deutsche marks for souvenirs. They were worthless, as the Allied Occupation Currency replaced them. I'm sure when the American sergeant who operated the black market at Ziegenhain found this out, he was fit to be tied.

We received a thirty-day furlough at home, which was nice. My parents had a Christmas tree waiting for me in May. Afterward, we POWs spent thirty days at the Lake Placid resort in upstate New York. There we were interviewed and examined, both physically and psychologically, while having a wonderful vacation. Ed Sullivan, then a reporter for a New York newspaper, interviewed me. People wanted to know about us.

I refused the Purple Heart; there was no way I could wear it for just a scratch on the nose. In November 1945, I was discharged from the military hospital at Fort Dix. The diagnosis was a herniated disk in my spine. It had ruptured when the guard hit me with his rifle butt. The silver crucifix remains on the chain around my neck; each December 16, when I have pancakes, bacon, and strawberry jam, I wonder where the time has gone and ask myself if it was all really worth it.

In combat, I was so relieved when I lost my fear and became a soldier: I was relieved once again when this feeling passed. I got drunk a few times remembering the friend I left in the foxhole in Luxembourg. My fiancée understood why I was drunk; she wanted to understand what I felt. I answered, "Helpless." Eventually this also passed.

In January 1946, I returned to Gettysburg College to get on with my life.

It had changed.

On May 21, 2004, I appeared on the History Channel during an hour segment titled "The Bridge at Arnhem." Christian Frey, producer, German History Channel, created a six-hour documentary titled "War of the Century," for the German people. The government wanted the German people to understand this war from the mouths of both German and American soldiers who had fought one another. Upon its completion, the producer gave this documentary to the American History Channel. I narrated this particular segment covering the two campaigns: the Battle of the Huertgen Forest and the Battle of the Bulge.

After reading this manuscript in Germany, Christian telephoned me in the summer of 2003 and asked permission for a July on-camera interview at my home in Columbia, South Carolina.

Shortly thereafter I met him, spoke on camera for two and a half hours, and over some German beer we began a warm friendship. Mike Dawson, writer of this book's introduction, accompanied me, as it was his prodding and excellent military knowledge that enabled me to write this work. I am forever grateful to him and to Christian.

Home from the war. Harrisburg, Pennsylvania, 1945.

Meller at Gettysburg College in Pennsylvania, 1947.